# Workbook 12

# Developing Yourself and Your Staff

Manage People
Certificate
S/NVQ Level 4

Institute of Management and Open Learning Programme

Series editor: Gareth Lewis
Author: Lisa Davis

chartered

management

institute

Pergamon
*Flexible*
Learning

Pergamon Flexible Learning
An imprint of Elsevier Science
Linacre House, Jordan Hill, Oxford OX2 8DP
200 Wheeler Road, Burlington,MA 01830

First published 1997
Reprinted 1999, 2000, 2001, 2002, 2003

**British Library Cataloguing in Publication Data**
A catalogue record for this book is available from the British Library

ISBN 0 7506 3670 X

For more information on all Butterworth-Heineman publications
please visit our website at www.bh.com

Typeset by Avocet Typeset, Brill, Aylesbury, Bucks
Printed and bound in Great Britain

# Contents

# Series overview

The Institute of Management Open Learning Programme is a series of workbooks prepared by the Institute of Management and Pergamon Open Learning for managers seeking to develop themselves.

Comprising seventeen open learning workbooks, the programme covers the best of modern management theory and practice, and each workbook provides a range of frameworks and techniques to improve your effectiveness as a manager, thus helping you acquire the knowledge and skill to make you fully competent in your role.

Each workbook is written by an experienced management writer and covers an important management topic or theme. The activities both reinforce learning and help to relate the generic ideas to your individual work context. While coverage of each topic is fully comprehensive, additional reading suggestions and reference sources are given for those who wish to study to a greater depth.

Designed to be practical, stimulating and challenging, the aim of the workbooks is to improve performance at work by benefiting you and your organization. This practical focus is at the heart of the competence based approach that has been adopted by the programme.

## The structure of the programme

The design and overall structure of the programme has two main organizing principles, both of which are closely linked to the national standards for management developed by the MCI (Management Charter Initiative).

First, the workbooks are grouped according to the key roles of management.

- Underpinning the management standards are a series of **personal competences** which describe the personal skills required by all managers, which are essential to skill in all the main functional or key role areas.
- **Manage Activities** describes the principles of managing processes and activities, with service to the customer as an essential part of this.
- **Manage Resources** describes the acquisition, control and monitoring of financial and other resources.
- **Manage People** looks at the key skills involved in leadership, developing one's staff and managing their performance.

■ **Manage Information** discusses the acquisition, storage and use of information for communication, problem solving and decision making.

In addition, there are three specialized key roles: **Manage Quality, Manage Projects** and **Manage Energy**. The workbooks cover the first two of these. Unlike the four primary key roles above, these are not compulsory for certificate, diploma or S/NVQ requirements, but provide options for the latter.

Together, these key roles provide a comprehensive description of the fundamental principles of management as it applies in any organization – commercial, maintained sector or not-for-profit.

Second, the programme is organized according to **levels of management**, seniority and responsibility.

Level 4 represents first line management. In accredited programmes this is equivalent to S/NVQ Level 4, Certificate in Management or CMS. Level 5 is equivalent to middle/senior management and is accredited at S/NVQ Level 5, Diploma in Management or DMS. There are two S/NVQs at Level 5: Operational Management and Strategic Management. The operations role is focussed internally within an organization on the maintenance of systems and standards of output, whilst the strategic role is focussed on the whole organization, including the external operating environment, and looks at setting directions.

Together, the workbooks cover all the background knowledge you need to have for all units of competence in the MCI standards at Level 4 and Level 5 (apart from the specialized units in the key role Manage Energy). They also provide skills development and opportunities for portfolio building.

For a comprehensive list of workbooks, see page ix. For a comprehensive list of links with the standards, see the *User Guide*.

## How to use the programme

The programme is deliberately designed to be flexible and can be used in a variety of ways:

■ to update on important management topics and themes, or develop individual skills: as the workbooks are grouped according to themes, it should be easy for you to pick out one that suits your needs

■ as part of generic management development programmes: you can choose the modules that fit the themes of the programme

■ as part of, and in support of, accredited competence-based programmes.

For N/SVQs at both Levels 4 and 5, there are options in the combinations of units that make up the various awards. By using the map provided in the *User Guide*, individuals will be able to select the workbooks appropriate to their specific needs, and their chosen accreditation options. Some of the activities will help you provide evidence for your portfolio; where we think this is the case, we give the relevant reference to the standards.

For Certificate or CMS, Diploma or DMS, individuals should choose modules that not only meet their individual needs but also satisfy the requirements of the delivering body and the awarding body.

You may need help and guidance in these choices, and the *User Guide* sets out the options and advice in much more detail. A fuller description of the potential uses of this material in evidence gathering and portfolio building can also be found in the *User Guide*, as can a detailed description of the contents of each workbook.

# Workbooks in the Institute of Management Open Learning Programme

Manage People (Level 5)

14 *The New Model Leader*

Manage Information (Level 4)

15 *Making Rational Decisions*
16 *Communication*

Manage Information (Level 5)

17 *Successful Information Management*

Manage Quality (Level 4)

3 *Understanding Business Process Management**
4 *Customer Focus**

Manage Quality (Level 5)

5 *Getting TQM to Work**

Manage Projects (Level 4)

8 *Project Management**

Manage Projects (Level 5)

8 *Project Management**

Support Materials

18 *User Guide*
19 *Mentor Guide*

An asterisk indicates that a particular workbook also contains material suitable for a particular key role or personal competence.

# Links to qualifications

This unit is directly relevant to Unit C9, Develop teams and individuals to enhance performance.

Specifically:

C9.1  Identify training and development needs for teams and individuals
C9.2  Plan the training and development of teams and individuals
C9.3  Develop teams to improve performance
C9.4  Support individual learning and development
C9.5  Assess teams and individuals against training and development objectives
C9.6  Improve development activities

## S/NVQ programmes

This workbook can help candidates to achieve credit and develop skills in the key role managing people at level 4, and covers the following units and elements:

C10  Develop teams and indivduals to enhance performance
C10.1  Identify the development needs of teams and individuals
C10.2  Plan the development of teams and individuals
C10.3  Develop teams to improve performance
C10.4  Support individual learning and development
C10.5  Assess the development of teams and individuals
C10.6  Improve the development of teams and individuals

## Certificate and Diploma programmes

This workbook, together with the Level 4 workbooks on managing people (1 – *The Influential Manager*, 2 – *Managing Yourself*, 11 – *Getting the Right People to do the Right Job* and 13 – *Building a High Performance Team*) covers all of the knowledge required in the key role Manage People for Certificate in Management and CMS programmes.

# Links to other workbooks

Other workbooks in the key role Manage People at Level 4 are:

1  *The Influential Manager*
2  *Managing Yourself*
11  *Getting the Right People to do the Right Job*
13  *Building a High Performance Team*

and at Level 5:

14  *The New Model Leader*

# Introduction

**Personal** development is a two-stage process. It begins with discovering as much as you can about yourself, your needs, your preferences and your hopes for the future. And the second stage is about choosing to take responsibility for acquiring new skills and knowledge, making changes and, generally, taking control of your life so that you can achieve your full potential and move towards the future you want for yourself.

**Staff** development is about working with other people to enable them, through a range of different learning opportunities such as structured training, coaching and mentoring, to achieve their full potential.

This workbook focuses on the techniques and processes you can use for your own personal development, and for developing the people you work with through:

- designing and delivering appropriate training
- coaching on a one-to-one basis
- acting as a mentor and wise adviser

However, the detailed treatment of team development is contained in Workbook 13, *Building a High Performance Team*.

## Objectives

By the end of this workbook you should be able to:

- identify any areas of personal or professional development you would like to work on
- identify your own preferred learning style
- identify your specific personal goals for the future
- carry out a SWOT analysis on your career
- conduct a training needs analysis
- implement Investors in People within your organization
- list the key factors that enable learners to learn
- recognize the difference between:
    - an effective and an ineffective trainer/facilitator
    - an effective and an ineffective training event
- use a range of techniques to coach people and develop teams in order to improve performance
- act as a mentor

# Section 1 Personal development

## Introduction

Personal development is an ongoing process which, for many people, continues throughout life. Unlike career development, which is often a fairly straightforward path from point A to point B, the route to personal development can be convoluted, complex and, often, surprising.

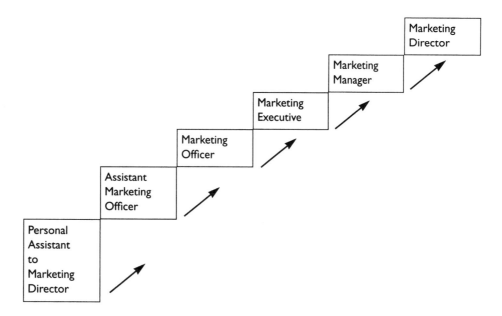

**Figure 1**   Example of a career development path

For some people personal development means acquiring new skills and knowledge – anything from book-binding to yacht racing to understanding chaos theory. For others, it involves widening their social circle and becoming involved in community activities. For some people it is about spiritual development, and for some it relates to a deeper understanding of science and technology, or the world, and their place within it.

The first section of this workbook is designed to help you think about what personal development means for you and how you can identify those areas where you would like to make changes or improvements.

Once we understand the broader principles and techniques involved in self-development, we can help to apply them for the benefit of others.

| 1991 moved to the cottage | | 1987 bought Time Share in Spain | 1990 took 'A' level Spanish | 1993 sold Time Share – bought house in Spain |
|---|---|---|---|---|
| 1992 garden completed | **M E** | | | |
| 1993 selling home-grown veg. to the local shop | | 1989 damaged back in car crash | 1990 started Yoga classes | 1991 started meditation classes |
| 1996 bought an acre of land to extend market garden | | | | 1993 started to study for British Wheel of Yoga exams |
| | | | | 1996 qualified as a Yoga teacher |

**Figure 2**   Example of a personal development path

# What is personal development?

Personal development means different things to different people. Here is what a group of European managers said in response to the question 'How would you define personal development?'

■  'It's about developing self awareness. Personal development is the process of coming to understand yourself – knowing how you tick and what you do best.' 'I think personal development is about stretching yourself – not just in relation to the job, but in relation to every aspect of life. Relationships, money, health – everything.'

■  'It's about getting to be as good as you can be at what you want to do – so personal development relates to job skills, people skills, communication skills, I think.'

■  'Personal development, for me, has always been about expanding my horizons through travel and reading and meeting people. It's about being open to new ideas, taking risks, being willing to look at things in a new way. Whenever I feel I'm getting stuck in a rut I deliberately set myself a challenge. Last year it was learning to speak Spanish, and this year I've taken up rock climbing. Every challenge helps me to gain new skills but, most of all, gain confidence in myself and my abilities.'

- 'Personal development, for me, is knowing more this year than I knew last year.'
- 'It's about knowing myself better – what I like, what I do well, what I'm capable of – and then arranging my life to suit me.'

The following activity provides an opportunity for you define what Personal Development means to you.

## ACTIVITY 1

What does personal development mean to you in the context of your life, your goals and your ambitions? Take as long as you need to consider this question and then complete the sentence below.

For me, personal development is

## FEEDBACK

There is no right or wrong answer to this question because everyone is different and has different interests, opinions, values and beliefs. Even so, for most people, personal development is about one or more of the following:

- developing greater self-knowledge and understanding
- acquiring new skills and/or knowledge (which may or may not be job related)
- setting and meeting personal goals

The remainder of this section is designed to help you to examine each of these key areas within your own life.

# Self awareness

Developing self-knowledge and understanding is a key aspect of the self-development process. Take as long as you need to complete the next activity and be sure to answer each question as honestly as possible. You might want to write your answers on a separate sheet of paper to preserve confidentiality.

## ACTIVITY 2

### Self-awareness area 1: Professional knowledge

1 How do you keep up to date with current thinking in your own specialism or area of expertise?

How could you improve?

2 How do you keep abreast of the latest management techniques and ideas?

How could you improve?

3 Is there someone in your professional life who informally acts as your mentor and 'wise adviser'?

If not, who would be acceptable to you in this role? How might you persuade them to take on this role?

### Self-awareness area 2: Sensitivity to people and situations

1 What type of situations do you find most difficult to weigh up?

2 What kind of people, generally, cause most problems for you?

3 Do you tend to tune in to people and situations and proceed on intuition and gut feeling? Or do you respond after careful analysis and deliberation, basing your reactions on logic?

4 What, usually, causes you to make assumptions (and judgements) about people and/or situations?

How do you check out whether or not your assumptions are correct?

### Self-awareness area 3: Decision making

1 On a scale of 1 to 10 (where 1 is low and 10 is high), how comfortable and confident are you about making:

|   | 1 | 2 | 3 | 4 | 5 | 6 | 7 | 8 | 9 | 10 |
|---|---|---|---|---|---|---|---|---|---|----|
| a personal decisions: | ❑ | ❑ | ❑ | ❑ | ❑ | ❑ | ❑ | ❑ | ❑ | ❑ |
| b business decisions: | ❑ | ❑ | ❑ | ❑ | ❑ | ❑ | ❑ | ❑ | ❑ | ❑ |

2 Specifically, what kind of decisions are most difficult for you, and why?

3 How could you improve?

### Self-awareness area 4: Interpersonal skills

1 On a scale of 1 to 10 (where 1 is low and 10 is high), how would you rate your:

| | | | | | | | | | | |
|---|---|---|---|---|---|---|---|---|---|---|
| a self-confidence? | ❑ | ❑ | ❑ | ❑ | ❑ | ❑ | ❑ | ❑ | ❑ | ❑ |
| b self-esteem? | ❑ | ❑ | ❑ | ❑ | ❑ | ❑ | ❑ | ❑ | ❑ | ❑ |
| c assertiveness? | ❑ | ❑ | ❑ | ❑ | ❑ | ❑ | ❑ | ❑ | ❑ | ❑ |
| d communication skills? | ❑ | ❑ | ❑ | ❑ | ❑ | ❑ | ❑ | ❑ | ❑ | ❑ |

Where necessary, how can you improve?

2 Which kinds of people do you find easiest to manage, and why?

3 Which kinds of people do you find most difficult to manage, and why?

### Self-awareness area 5: Stress management

1 What kinds of situations and people upset you and stress you the most?

2 With which people and in which situations do you feel most in control?

3 What positive steps (if any) do you currently take to manage the stress in your life?

How might you improve?

**Self-awareness Area 6: Proactivity**

1   In which kinds of situations are you most likely to take the initiative, and why?

2   In which kinds of situations are you least likely to take the initiative, and why?

3   What positive steps could you take to become more proactive:
    a   at home?

    b   at work?

**Self-awareness area 7: Creativity and flexibility**

1   What techniques do you use to generate new ideas and/or creative solutions?

2   What do you do when faced with apparently contradictory information or requirements?

3   How do you cope when you are required to deal with a multitude of tasks or ideas, or problems or situations?

How could you improve?

## FEEDBACK

The answers to these questions will, of course, be highly personal and relate to the way in which you, as an individual, operate and function. There are, of course, no right or wrong responses but, hopefully, the answers you have given may have highlighted, for you, some areas where you might benefit from directing your attention.

Use the next activity to help you to check out your Need to Achieve. This should be interpreted as your need to achieve success and excellence in most of the things you do.

## ACTIVITY 3[1]

Consider each pair of statements in the chart below and then tick the appropriate box: a, b, c, d or e, where a = Yes, absolutely; b = I suppose so; c = In between; d = I suppose so; e = Yes, absolutely.

For example: Question 1: If your response is YES, ABSOLUTELY to the right-hand statement – I prefer to tackle tasks which present a challenge and which require me to do a lot of hard thinking, then tick column e.

|  | a | b | c | d | e |  |
|---|---|---|---|---|---|---|
| 1 I prefer to handle tasks which I know I can complete well, without too much difficulty |  |  |  |  | ✓ | I prefer to tackle tasks which present a challenge and which require me to do a lot of hard thinking |

|  | a | b | c | d | e |  |
|---|---|---|---|---|---|---|
| 1 I prefer to handle tasks which I know I can complete well, without too much difficulty |  |  |  |  |  | I prefer to tackle tasks which present a challenge and which require me to do a lot of hard thinking |
| 2 I prefer to have frequent opportunities to check and measure my progress |  |  |  |  |  | I prefer not to do tests, and would prefer not to have to check my progress against test results |
| 3 I prefer to work at my own pace and set my own deadlines |  |  |  |  |  | I prefer it if the pace of work is dictated by others, and deadlines are set for me |
| 4 I prefer being able to manage my workload without constantly stretching myself |  |  |  |  |  | I prefer having to constantly stretch myself to achieve successful completion of my workload |
| 5 I prefer to know exactly what I have to do, how to do it, and what results I need to achieve |  |  |  |  |  | I prefer to be able to exercise my own initiative and judgement to decide what to do, how to do it and what results I need to achieve |

| | a | b | c | d | e | |
|---|---|---|---|---|---|---|
| 6 I prefer to begin new projects without too much lead time, and to focus on one project at a time | | | | | | I prefer to have plenty of advance warning about new projects so I can plan ahead; and I prefer to work on several projects at one time |
| 7 I prefer to set my own targets and adjust my performance depending on the results I'm achieving | | | | | | I prefer to work to clearly defined targets and goal-posts that are not constantly being moved. |

Compare your scores with the scores in the box below, and then total the figures. E.g. If you ticked box e for question I score 5 points.

| | a | b | c | d | e | |
|---|---|---|---|---|---|---|
| I I prefer to handle tasks which I know I can complete well, without too much difficulty | I | 2 | 3 | 4 | 5 | I prefer to tackle tasks which present a challenge and which require me to do a lot of hard thinking |
| 2 I prefer to have frequent opportunities to check and measure my progress | 5 | 4 | 3 | 2 | I | I prefer not to do tests, and would prefer not to have to check my progress against test results |
| 3 I prefer to work at my own pace and set my own deadlines | 5 | 4 | 3 | 2 | I | I prefer it if the pace of work is dictated by others, and deadlines are set for me |
| 4 I prefer being able to manage my workload so I can succeed without constantly stretching myself | I | 2 | 3 | 4 | 5 | I prefer having to constantly stretch myself to achieve success |

| | a | b | c | d | e | |
|---|---|---|---|---|---|---|
| 5 I prefer to know exactly what I have to do, how to do it, and what results I need to achieve | 1 | 2 | 3 | 4 | 5 | I prefer to be able to exercise my own initiative and judgement to decide what to do, how to do it and what results I need to achieve |
| 6 I prefer to begin new projects without too much lead time, and to focus on one project at a time | 1 | 2 | 3 | 4 | 5 | I prefer to have plenty of advance warning about new projects so I can plan ahead; and I prefer to work on several projects at one time |
| 7 I prefer to set my own targets and adjust my performance depending on the results I'm achieving | 5 | 4 | 3 | 2 | 1 | I prefer to work to clearly defined targets and goal-posts that are not constantly being moved. |

Total score _____

**Scoring results**

Neither High nor Low scores are Good or Bad. Your score simply reflects one part of your personality and one aspect of the way in which you relate to the world.

If you scored **31 or more** you have a strong need to achieve. You are competitive, highly motivated and prefer to work alone.
If you scored **26 to 30** your need to achieve is slightly higher than average. Although a good team player when necessary, you value your independence.
If you scored **20 to 25** your need to achieve is about average. You like to operate in a fairly structured environment, without too many surprises.
If you scored **15 to 19** your need to achieve is slightly below average. You are most comfortable when you know what it is you have to do, and you feel confident that you will be able to do it well.
If you scored **below 15** your need to achieve is definitely below average. Your attitude to work and life in general is very relaxed and non-competitive.

The next activity will enable you to consider whether or not your current lifestyle offers you sufficient new challenges to satisfy your need to achieve.

## ACTIVITY 4

Consider each of the following questions and tick the appropriate box.

| | Most of the time | Some of the time | Rarely | Never |
|---|---|---|---|---|
| 1 My working life provides me with tasks which offer me sufficient challenges and mental stimulation | | | | |
| 2 I have hobbies or interests outside of work which provide me with challenges and mental stimulation | | | | |
| 3 At work there are sufficient opportunities available to me to allow me to check and measure my progress | | | | |
| 4 I create opportunities, outside of work, which allow me to check and measure my abilities or progress | | | | |
| 5 At work I am comfortable with the pace at which I work and the way in which deadlines are set | | | | |
| 6 Outside of work I am involved in activities where I am comfortable with the pace at which I work and the way in which deadlines are set | | | | |
| 7 At work I feel sufficiently stretched and challenged | | | | |
| 8 I have leisure time interests and hobbies which stretch and challenge me | | | | |
| 9 I am comfortable with the way in which I am free to use sufficient initiative and judgement at work | | | | |
| 10 In my life outside of work I am involved in activities which require me to use my initiative and judgement to the degree which suits me best | | | | |

|  | Most of the time | Some of the time | Rarely | Never |
|---|---|---|---|---|
| 11 At work, projects provide me with sufficient challenges and stimulation |  |  |  |  |
| 12 Outside of work I become involved in projects which offer me sufficient challenges and stimulation |  |  |  |  |
| 13 I am comfortable with the way in which my work goals and targets are defined and set |  |  |  |  |
| 14 Outside of work I become involved in interests and activities which provide me with goals which I find acceptable and achievable |  |  |  |  |

## FEEDBACK

Once again there are no Right or Wrong answers. Your responses to these questions simply reflect whether or not, in relation to your own personal Need to Achieve, there are sufficient challenges in your life, and a degree of mental stimulation appropriate for your needs.

For example, if you have ticked 'most of the time' in response to seven or more of the questions then your life is, generally, stimulating and challenging. Probably, either at work or in your leisure time, you are creating frequent opportunities for you to satisfy your Need to Achieve. If, though, you have ticked 'never' in response to seven or more of the questions, then it could be time to focus on ways in which you can begin to introduce the kinds of challenges you require in order to satisfy your Need to Achieve. In an activity a little further on in this section we will be looking at a technique you can use to set challenging, yet realistic goals in your life.

# Learning new skills and knowledge

The second key aspect of personal development is taking the opportunity to learn new skills and acquire new knowledge, either:

- in your working life
- in your life outside work
- both at work and in your own time

Understanding **how** you learn is equally as important as **what** you learn.

The next activity will give you an opportunity to help you to establish your own, personal, preferred learning style. Once you know how you prefer to learn, this will enable you then to make the most of any learning opportunities which become available.

## ACTIVITY 5[2]

Consider each of the statements in the chart below:

- If you **agree** with a statement **more** than you disagree, ✓ the Agree box.
- If you **disagree** with a statement **more** than you agree, ✗ the Disagree box.

| | Agree | Disagree |
|---|---|---|
| 1 I hold strong views and opinions about what is and what is not acceptable; what is good or bad, right or wrong | | |
| 2 I often throw caution to the wind | | |
| 3 I tend to solve problems using a logical, reasoned, step-by-step approach | | |
| 4 I believe that formal policies and procedures stamp out individuality and cramp people's style | | |
| 5 I have a reputation for being direct – I call a spade a spade, and people know it | | |
| 6 I often follow my gut-feeling and find that the results are just as sound as if I had used careful analysis and logical reasoning | | |
| 7 I like to get involved in the sort of work where I have time to 'leave no stone unturned' | | |
| 8 I regularly question people about their basic assumptions | | |
| 9 What matters most is whether or not something actually works in practice | | |
| 10 I actively seek out new experiences | | |
| 11 As soon as I hear about a new idea or approach I start thinking about how to apply it in practice | | |
| 12 I consider self-discipline is important – the ability to stick to a diet, take regular exercise, observe a fixed routine, and so on | | |

|  | Agree | Disagree |
|---|---|---|
| 13 I take pride in doing a thorough job |  |  |
| 14 I get on best with logical, analytical people and less well with spontaneous people who tend to hold irrational views |  |  |
| 15 I take care over the interpretation of data which is presented to me and avoid jumping to conclusions |  |  |
| 16 I reach decisions carefully, only after I have weighed up many alternatives |  |  |
| 17 I am attracted more to novel, unusual ideas – rather than practical ideas |  |  |
| 18 I don't like loose ends – I prefer to fit things into a coherent pattern |  |  |
| 19 I accept and stick to laid down procedures and policies so long as I regard them as an efficient way of getting the job done |  |  |
| 20 I like to relate my actions to general principle |  |  |
| 21 In discussions, I like to get straight to the point |  |  |
| 22 I tend to have distant, rather formal relationships with people at work |  |  |
| 23 I thrive on the challenge of tackling something new and different |  |  |
| 24 I enjoy fun-loving, spontaneous people |  |  |
| 25 I pay meticulous attention to detail before coming to a conclusion |  |  |
| 26 I find it difficult to come up with wild, off-the-top-of-my-head ideas |  |  |
| 27 I don't believe in wasting time by beating around the bush |  |  |
| 28 I am careful not to jump to conclusions too quickly |  |  |
| 29 I prefer to have as many sources of information as possible – as far as I'm concerned, the more data to mull over, the better |  |  |
| 30 Flippant people who don't take things seriously enough usually irritate me |  |  |
| 31 I listen to other people's points of view before putting my own forward |  |  |

| | Agree | Disagree |
|---|---|---|
| 32 I tend to be open about how I'm feeling | | |
| 33 In discussions I enjoy watching the manoeuvrings of the other participants | | |
| 34 I prefer to respond to events on a spontaneous, flexible basis, rather than plan things out in advance | | |
| 35 I tend to be attracted to techniques such as network analysis, flow charts, branching programmes, contingency planning and so on | | |
| 36 It worries me if I have to rush out a piece of work to meet a tight deadline | | |
| 37 I tend to judge people's ideas on their practical merits | | |
| 38 Quiet, thoughtful people tend to make me feel uneasy | | |
| 39 I often get irritated by people who want to run headlong into things | | |
| 40 It's more important to enjoy the present than to think about the past or the future | | |
| 41 I think that decisions based on a thorough analysis of all the information are sounder than those based on intuition | | |
| 42 I tend to be a perfectionist | | |
| 43 In discussions, I usually pitch in with lots of off-the-top-of-my-head ideas | | |
| 44 In meetings I try to put forward practical, realistic ideas | | |
| 45 More often than not, rules are there to be broken | | |
| 46 I prefer to stand back from a situation and consider all of the perspectives | | |
| 47 I can often see inconsistencies and weaknesses in other people's arguments | | |
| 48 On balance, I talk more than I listen | | |
| 49 I can often see better, more practical ways of getting things done | | |
| 50 I think that written reports should be short, punchy and to the point | | |
| 51 I believe that rational, logical thinking should win the day | | |

| | Agree | Disagree |
|---|---|---|
| 52 I tend to discuss specific things with people, rather than engaging in small talk | | |
| 53 I like people who have both feet firmly on the ground | | |
| 54 In discussions, I get impatient with irrelevances and red herrings | | |
| 55 If I have a report to write, I tend to produce numerous drafts before settling on a final version | | |
| 56 I am keen to try things out to see if they work in practice | | |
| 57 I am keen to reach answers via a logical approach | | |
| 58 I enjoy being the one that talks a lot | | |
| 59 In discussions, I often find that I am the realist, keeping people to the point and avoiding flights of fancy and wild speculation | | |
| 60 I like to ponder many alternatives before making up my mind | | |
| 61 In discussions with people I often find that I am the most dispassionate and objective | | |
| 62 In discussions, I'm more likely to adopt a low profile, rather than take the lead and do most of the talking | | |
| 63 I like to be able to relate current actions to the longer term, bigger picture | | |
| 64 When things go wrong, I'm happy to shrug it off and put it down to experience | | |
| 65 I tend to reject wild, off-the-top-of-the head ideas as being impractical | | |
| 66 It's better to look before you leap | | |
| 67 On balance, I do the listening rather than the talking | | |
| 68 I tend to be tough on people who find it difficult to adopt a logical approach | | |
| 69 Most times, I believe that the end justifies the means | | |
| 70 I don't mind hurting people's feelings so long as the job gets done | | |
| 71 I find the formality of having specific objectives and plans stifling | | |

|  | Agree | Disagree |
|---|---|---|
| 72 I'm usually the life and soul of the party |  |  |
| 73 I do whatever is expedient to get the job done |  |  |
| 74 I quickly get bored with methodical, detailed work |  |  |
| 75 I am keen on exploring the basic assumptions, principles and theories underpinning things and events |  |  |
| 76 I'm always interested to find out what other people think |  |  |
| 77 I like meetings to be run on methodical lines, sticking to laid down agendas and so on |  |  |
| 78 I steer clear of subjective or ambiguous topics |  |  |
| 79 I enjoy the drama and excitement of a crisis situation |  |  |
| 80 People often find me insensitive to their feelings |  |  |

## Checking your score

To determine your preferred learning style:

- ignore all the crosses you marked in the Disagree column
- in the lists below, circle the numbers that match the questions you marked with a tick in the Agree column
- score one point for each tick
- total the ticks in each list. The list with the highest score of ticks indicates your preferred learning style

| List A | List B | List C | List D |
|---|---|---|---|
| 2 | 7 | 1 | 5 |
| 4 | 13 | 3 | 9 |
| 6 | 15 | 8 | 11 |
| 10 | 16 | 12 | 19 |
| 17 | 25 | 14 | 21 |
| 23 | 28 | 18 | 27 |
| 24 | 29 | 20 | 35 |
| 32 | 31 | 22 | 37 |

| List A | List B | List C | List D |
|--------|--------|--------|--------|
| 34 | 33 | 26 | 44 |
| 38 | 36 | 30 | 49 |
| 40 | 39 | 42 | 50 |
| 43 | 41 | 47 | 53 |
| 45 | 46 | 51 | 54 |
| 48 | 52 | 57 | 56 |
| 58 | 55 | 61 | 59 |
| 64 | 60 | 63 | 65 |
| 71 | 62 | 68 | 69 |
| 72 | 66 | 75 | 70 |
| 74 | 67 | 77 | 73 |
| 79 | 76 | 78 | 80 |
| Score: | Score: | Score: | Score: |

## FEEDBACK

- If you scored most ticks in List A, then you are an Activist Learner.
- If you scored most ticks in List B, then you are a Reflective Learner.
- If you scored most ticks in List C, then you are a Theoretical Learner.
- If you scored most ticks in List D, then you are a Pragmatist Learner.

## ACTIVIST LEARNERS

If you are an Activist Learner you probably enjoy taking risks, and learning from trial and error. You accept that you are likely to make mistakes during the learning process, and you make sure you learn from them. It's very important for you to be actively involved in the learning process.

You will learn best from:

- handling problems, dealing with crises, tackling new challenges and experiences
- exciting and dramatic situations where circumstances chop and change and there are opportunities for you to become involved in a range of diverse activities
- getting involved in situations with other people where you can bounce ideas around, and solve problems through teamwork
- situations where you have high visibility – chairing meetings, leading discussions, making presentations and so on

- group learning activities such as business games, competitive teamwork tasks and role-playing exercises

You will learn least from (and may even react against):

- getting involved in assimilating, analysing and interpreting lots of 'messy' data
- having to engage in solitary activities such as reading, writing or thinking on your own
- situations where you have to stand back and not get involved
- formal learning activities such as listening to lectures, reading or watching someone perform a task

## REFLECTIVE LEARNERS

If you are a Reflective Learner you will, generally, prefer to watch and listen before getting involved. You dislike being thrown in at the deep end and appreciate being able to take things step by step, reflecting on what has been learned at each stage of the process.

You will learn best from:

- situations where you have ample time in which to prepare in advance so you can assimilate information, mull it over and think things through before you are required to take action or give an opinion
- situations that require painstaking research, giving you the opportunity to investigate and gather data
- preparing carefully considered and analysed reports
- watching other people perform tasks and then thinking about and chewing over what you have seen

You will learn least from (and may even react against):

- situations where, in the interest of expediency, you have to take short-cuts or produce superficial work
- situations in which, worried about time pressures, you rush from one task to another, desperately trying to meet deadlines
- being required to make decisions or reach conclusions which are based on insufficient data
- being forced into the limelight and having to chair a meeting, lead a discussion or role-play in front of other people

## THEORETICAL LEARNERS

If you are a Theoretical Learner you will feel most comfortable dealing with facts, figures and abstract ideas. You like to know **why** you are doing something and **how** things work.

You will learn best from:

- having sufficient time to explore, methodically, the associations and inter-relationships between ideas, events and situations
- having the opportunity to question the basic methodology which has been used, or probe the assumptions made and the logic used to reach conclusions
- being able to listen to or read about ideas and concepts based on rationality and logic; especially those that are watertight, elegant and well argued
- working with activities and tasks that are part of a system or model concept, or those based firmly upon an accepted theory

You will learn least from (and may even react against):

- being thrown in at the deep end and having to get involved in activities set in a clearly defined context, or with no clear purpose
- getting involved in situations (or structured learning activities) where there are high levels of ambiguity and uncertainty
- having to participate in situations where the emphasis is on emotions and feelings
- any activity, task or situation that you feel is shallow, superficial or gimmicky

## PRAGMATIST LEARNERS

If you are a Pragmatist Learner you need to know precisely what it is you are aiming to achieve. You appreciate being able to watch an expert at work and then try to emulate the style and actions of someone who really knows what they are doing. You most easily acquire new skills and knowledge through repetition; memorizing each word or repeating each action until you have it right.

You will learn best from:

- situations in which you can focus on practical issues and activities such as drawing up action plans or giving advice and assistance
- situations where you can obtain coaching and feedback from a credible expert
- learning opportunities where there is an obvious link between the subject matter and your own work, and where you can apply what you have learned in a practical way within your organization

You will learn least from (and may even react against):

- learning opportunities that seem to have no relevance to your job, your function or the issues of most concern to you
- situations, ideas, concepts that seem purely theoretical without any practical, useful application

- formal learning opportunities where there is no apparent reward, e.g. increased sales, more effective meetings, more professional presentations, increased opportunities for promotion, etc. to be gained.

Understanding your preferred learning style will help you choose the kind of learning opportunities to which you respond best.

# Setting and meeting personal goals

The third key aspect of ongoing personal development is connected to the process of life-planning and personal goals. For most people, having specific (and achievable) personal goals, gives their lives meaning and purpose. They have something to aim for and something to look forward to.

Personal goals can be:

- highly personal, e.g. Learn to ride a bicycle; Overcome my stutter; Lose 12lbs in weight
- career orientated, e.g. Stay £5000 under budget throughout the financial year; become Corporate Head by April; Move on to the Management Spine within two years
- financial, e.g. Pay sufficient into a Personal Pension Plan to give me 85 per cent of my salary when I retire; Save to buy a retirement home in Portugal; Start a Savings Plan for the children so there is additional money available for them when they go to University

Personal goals can be short, medium or long term (one week, six months, ten years); they can be small or large; easily achievable or require considerable effort, and possibly even sacrifice, to achieve. There are no right or wrong personal goals – each person sets their own targets according to their preferences, desires and needs.

Of course, some people never set personal goals because:

- I don't have time to think about the future
- planning ahead makes me nervous
- nothing has gone right so far, so why bother?
- setting goals is just tempting fate
- I'll feel a failure if I set goals and then don't achieve them

The keys to setting and achieving personal goals are:

1. making sure that your goal, target, objective or outcome (these words are all interchangeable and mean the same thing) are SMART. The acronym SMART represents:

Simple

Measurable

Achievable

Realistic

Time related

Setting SMART objectives is covered in detailed in Section 2 of Workbook 1, *Managing Yourself.*

2 breaking each large goal into a series of smaller, achievable steps. For example, Purchase a retirement home in Spain so I can move there in 2002:

Step 1 Investigate Spanish properties (1997)

Step 2 Sell boat to raise some capital for deposit (1997)

Step 3 Purchase property – irrespective of condition if the price and location are right (1997)

Step 4 Sell existing UK home and move to smaller property – reduced mortgage payments will support second mortgage in Spain (1997)

Step 5 Spend annual holidays in Spain preparing Spanish property for retirement (1998–2002)

The next activity will give you an opportunity to think about some personal goals you could set yourself for the future.

## ACTIVITY 6

**Part one**

Take as long as you need to think about your goals for the future. The goals could be related to highly personal achievements, finance, career, home and family, or anything else you choose.

In the chart below make a note of up to five goals, which could be short, medium or long term.

| Goal 1 | | Goal 3 | | Goal 5 |
| --- | --- | --- | --- | --- |
| | Goal 2 | | Goal 4 | |

**Part two**

For each goal you have identified in the chart above, note down the individual small steps you need to take which, when put together, will lead you to the achievement of your goal.

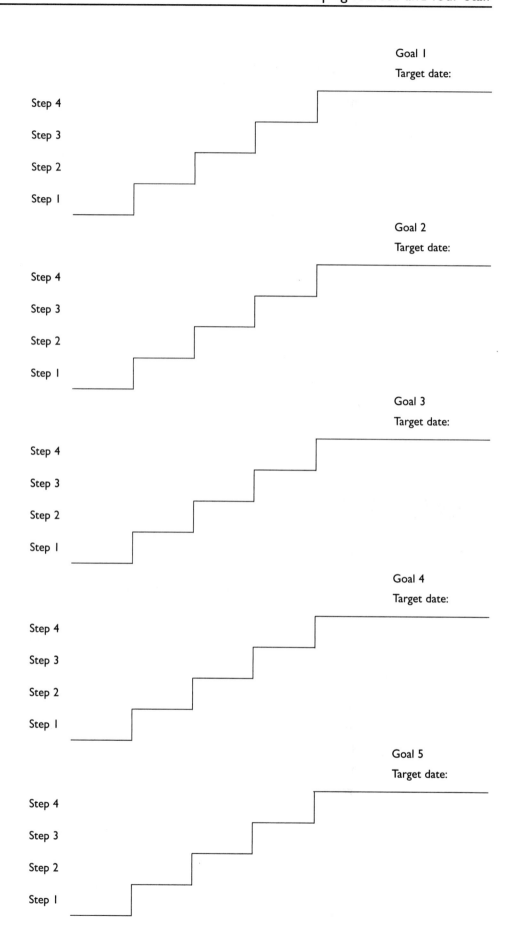

# Summary

- Personal Development is about:
    - developing greater self-knowledge and understanding
    - acquiring new skills and/or knowledge (which may or may not be job related)
    - setting and meeting personal goals
- Activist Learners learn from their mistakes, and prefer to be actively involved in the learning process – even if that means getting it hopelessly wrong at the start
- Reflective Learners prefer to learn 'step by step' and need time to consider what has been learned at each stage of the process
- Theoretical Learners like to know the reasons why they are doing something and how things work
- Pragmatist Learners acquire new skills and knowledge through repetition, memorizing words or repeating actions until they have got it right
- Personal Goals can be short, medium or long term. They can be small or large, easily achievable or require a great deal of effort. Whatever the Personal Goal is, it should be SMART:
    - Simple
    - Measurable
    - Achievable
    - Realistic
    - Time-related

and broken down into a series of small steps.

# Notes

[1] This quiz is based on the Henry A. Murray 'Need to Achieve' test; this version is adapted from *In the Know – 8 Keys to Successful Learning* by Martin Good and Christopher South (1988), pp. 26–27.

[2] This activity is based on the Learning Styles Questionnaire of Honey and Mumford in Wilcocks, G. and Morris, S. (1995) *Effective Manager*, Institute of Management/Pitman.

# Section 2  Career development

## Introduction

Some people plan their career with military precision. Most of us, though, stumble from job to job, taking advantage of the occasional opportunities which arise, and suddenly wake up to discover that retirement is, in fact, much closer than we thought.

Where you are right now in terms of your career development will depend on a number of personal factors, including your:

- age
- qualifications
- geographical location
- domestic circumstances

You may be perfectly happy with the way that your career is progressing and developing. Or, you may feel that now would be a good time to take stock of your current situation and seriously consider where you would like to be in five or ten years from now.

You can use the activities in this section to identify how you feel about your progress to date and, if necessary, create a career road-map for the future.

## PERSONAL SWOT ANALYSIS

Your hopes and goals for your **future** career development will depend, to a very large extent, on where you are **now**. Once you become clear about your current position, then you can begin to take a realistic look at the future.

The next activity will enable you to undertake a SWOT analysis to identify your Strengths and Weaknesses, together with the Opportunities available to you, and the Threats you may have to face. This will help you to see in which direction you should focus your energies for the future.

**ACTIVITY 7**

| Strengths | Weaknesses |
|---|---|
| ■ What qualifications do you have? <br> ■ Where does your experience lie? <br> ■ What specialist knowledge do you have? <br> ■ What skills, (including manual and artistic), do you have? <br> ■ What kind of a reputation do you have? <br> ■ What has help you most in your career to date? <br> ■ Who are your most influential contacts? <br> ■ What are the strong points of your character and personality? <br> ■ Under what circumstances have you felt the happiest and most fulfilled? <br> ■ Under what circumstances have you made the most valuable contribution? <br> ■ What support can you count on from family, friends and colleagues? <br> ■ Are there any other strengths you can add to the list? | ■ Are there any important gaps in your skills, knowledge, qualifications or experience? <br> ■ What financial difficulties or pressures do you face? <br> ■ Have you made any enemies? <br> ■ Do you, or anyone close to you, have health problems or disabilities and, if so, how does this affect you? <br> ■ What has hindered you most in your career to date? <br> ■ What are the weak points of your character and personality? <br> ■ Under what circumstances have you felt most frustrated and unhappy? <br> ■ Do your domestic circumstances limit in any way? <br> ■ Are there other limitations in your life? <br> ■ In what way do you consider yourself to be most vulnerable? <br> ■ Are there any other limitations you can add to the list? |
| Opportunities | Threats |
| ■ Are suitable job vacancies currently available, or likely to occur in the near future? <br> ■ Is there a re-structuring or re-organization likely which might offer a suitable opening? <br> ■ Are there gaps or niches in the market which you might be able to exploit? <br> ■ Have rivals or competitors difficulties or weaknesses which you might be able to exploit? <br> ■ Are there any consultancy opportunities available to you? <br> ■ Are there any writing, speaking or media opportunities available to you? <br> ■ Are there are grants or bursaries available, or any sponsorship opportunities? | ■ Forthcoming changes to legislation or regulations? <br> ■ Taxation or benefit changes? <br> ■ Likely loss of image or reputation? <br> ■ Possibility of financial or legal problems? <br> ■ Possibility of changes to European, national or local economy? <br> ■ Ill health – yourself or others? <br> ■ Rivalry or opposition from others? <br> ■ Obsolescence of your skills and knowledge? |

## FEEDBACK

Once your SWOT analysis is complete, your next step should be to consider, very carefully, what it is you really want from your career in the future.

## ACTIVITY 8

Consider the following questions and answer them honestly (using a separate sheet of paper if you prefer, to ensure confidentiality).

1   From the list below identify the factors that are most important to you, and that you most want to preserve or acquire in your life:

- security                                        ❑
- increased financial rewards                     ❑
- job satisfaction                                ❑
- ethical business practices                      ❑
- freedom and independence                        ❑
- challenging opportunities                        ❑
- different lifestyle                             ❑
- consolidation of existing lifestyle             ❑
- increased status and prestige                   ❑

2

a   Where do you see yourself in the short term (within six – twelve months)?

b   Where do you see yourself in the medium term (two – ten years)?

c   Where do you see yourself in the long term (ten – twenty years)?

d   Do your visions of the future include the factors you identified in question 1?

## FEEDBACK

Depending on your responses to the last activity you may have reached the conclusion that your career is absolutely on track and no changes or adjustments are necessary. On the other hand, you may now be thinking that some adjustments are required in order to get you where you want to be in five or ten years time. Your options for change are likely to be to:

- make big changes in one or more areas of your life and work
- make small changes in one or more areas of your life and work
- to plan ahead, so that the changes take place over a fairly long period of time
- act quickly and begin to make changes straight away

Your strategy for change may involve a complete change of direction, making changes within your current job or even changing some aspect of yourself.

## COMPLETE CHANGE OF DIRECTION

This is a major step and requires careful thought and planning. Some key points to take into consideration include:

- are there gaps in your skills, experience or qualifications? If so, how can you plug these gaps and acquire the necessary skills, experience or qualifications?
- do you have the financial resources necessary to enable you to make your desired change? If not, how can you acquire the necessary financial resources?
- do you have the support of family and friends? If not, what is their resistance to your desired change? How can you overcome this resistance?

## MAKING CHANGES WITHIN YOUR CURRENT JOB

Some realistic changes you could consider include:

- negotiate for a redefinition of your job to provide more challenging opportunities
- initiate a new project
- actively seek alternative ways of doing things
- investigate the options of relocation, job-share, part-time or flexible employment

## CHANGING YOURSELF

If, on reflection, you may feel that some aspect of yourself needs to change. The change required might be, say, for you to entertain more realistic expectations, or set more ambitious goals or even redefine your attitudes to work and career. You might like to think about:

- organizing training or education for yourself to update existing skills and knowledge, or acquire new areas of expertise
- seeking advice from a respected colleague or friend
- encouraging constructive feedback on your performance
- consulting a professional careers adviser

Whatever your choices and decisions, the key point to remember is that you are in the driving seat and, unless you actively initiate the changes you want, they are unlikely to happen.

Before you make any changes, do:

1   Use the same logical and analytical approach to considering your career as you would take to any other problem-solving or decision-making scenario.

2   Base your career decisions on careful research and valid information, and don't take risks.

3   Apply all of your management skills and competences to the management of your career.

4   Regularly monitor and review the situation and, where necessary, take appropriate remedial action.

5   Seek advice, feedback and discussion with a trusted mentor, colleague or friend.

## Summary

- A SWOT analysis will enable you to identify the:
  - Strengths
  - Weaknesses
  - Opportunities
  - Threats

  which may help or hinder you, either in your current career situation or in the future.
- When considering your options for change, your strategy may involve making:
  - long-term changes which will involve planning and foresight
  - immediate changes which need to be implemented quickly
  - changes within your current job, or with your current organization
  - a fresh start in a completely new direction
  - changing an important aspect of yourself
- Once you are clear about the changes you want, it is your responsibility to initiate the changes, and make them happen.
- Before you make any changes:
  - get clear about what it is you really want
  - avoid risk taking and make informed choices
- Always:
  - apply your management skills to managing your career
  - review and update your career plan on a regular basis

# Section 3 Analysing staff development needs

## Introduction

Before you can start the process of actually meeting staff development needs, it's important to find out precisely what those needs are. The old philosophy of 'Let's throw some money at the problem. If we give them some training that'll sort it out' is both outdated and totally unproductive.

Training should be carefully planned and meticulously organized to meet the real needs of both the individual and the organization. Anything less is patronizing to the staff, and financially wasteful for the company.

Training Needs Analysis which, it has to be said, is a time-consuming process, is the task of finding out:

- what people already know and can do
- what people need to know and do if they are to improve their job performance

In this section of the workbook we will be focusing on the ways in which you can identify genuine staff training needs.

## The benefits of staff development

As a manager one of your key tasks is to facilitate, in whatever way is most appropriate, the development of the people in your team. In this context, your team means everyone in the business for whom you have some responsibility. This process may include the development of one or more of the following:

- skills
- knowledge
- attitudes

## ACTIVITY 9

a   List three benefits that an organization can expect to enjoy as a result of effectively developing their staff:

1

2

3

b   List three costs that an organization can expect to suffer as a result of not effectively developing their staff:

1

2

3

## FEEDBACK

The **benefits** of staff development include:

LESS

- down-time on plant and machinery
- wastage and breakages
- accidents
- drifting schedules
- failure to meet production targets
- over-spending on budgets

IMPROVED

- competitive advantage
- quality and customer service, both of which result in increased customer satisfaction and loyalty
- staff motivation
- communication
- team-working
- labour retention – because happy people stay in their jobs for a longer period of time

The **costs** of not undertaking staff development include:

FINANCIAL COSTS related to:

- down-time on plant and machinery, breakages and waste, disruption to production schedules and budgets
- staff absenteeism
- recruitment costs
- loss of competitive advantage

REPUTATION COSTS related to:

- on-site accidents
- poor quality and customer service
- disputes with unions and staff organizations

EFFICIENCY COSTS related to:

- poor internal and external communication
- ineffective team working
- low staff motivation and morale
- resistance to change
- lack of innovative ideas

The whole point of developing individual people and teams is to add value to the business, whatever the nature of the business might be. People who have regular, consistent opportunities to update their skills and knowledge and acquire new ones, and who are empowered to use their initiative, think for themselves and take responsibility for their actions will add value. This is because they will feel respected and appreciated, and they will recognize that they are making an important contribution to the success of the business.

# Informal and organic, or formal and structured development?

## INFORMAL AND ORGANIC STAFF DEVELOPMENT

This kind of staff development often occurs because a senior member of staff spots talent and potential in a more junior member of staff. The senior person may, in an informal way, encourage that talent and potential by offering significant development opportunities as and when they occur.

**CASE STUDY**

Barbara, a senior manager in a publishing house, explains:

*'I used to work as a Personal Assistant to a woman who seemed to think I was capable of doing much, much more ... her opinion, rather than mine, I have to say. She would give me tasks which I honestly believed I was incapable of doing – but I liked her enormously, and I didn't want to let her down. Also, I suppose part of me felt that if she thought I was capable of doing it, then maybe I could! Of course, as I successfully completed each new task my self-esteem grew. I began to see that I was more capable than I had believed  –  and that's when my confidence really kicked in and I became more ambitious. I owe everything to her, because of the opportunities she gave me to prove myself.'*

Providing people with meaningful development opportunities can be nerve-wracking and, if your judgement is poor, even dangerous. For example, statements like:

- 'I'd like you to chair the meeting'
- 'I want you to make the presentation in New York'
- 'OK – it's your project, you set up the budget and manage it'
- 'You negotiate with the client'

if not properly thought through, can provide someone with a perfect opportunity to wreak total havoc in a business. But, if you are sure of the person to whom you are delegating, and if you delegate properly – by setting clear parameters and monitoring carefully, but unobtrusively – these kinds of challenges can develop people rapidly. (For detailed information about delegation, see Workbook 14; *The New Model Leader*.)

## ACTIVITY 10

Take a few moments to reflect back over your own career to date before answering the following questions:

1   Who has been instrumental in providing development opportunities for you?

2   What were those development opportunities?

3   How has the successful completion of those development opportunities affected:

   a   you, as an individual?

   b   your career?

## FEEDBACK

Opportunities are crucial to both individual development, and the development of the organization. Generally, capable people who have potential will rise to the challenge. Of course you may make some errors of judgement over the years. But, if you start in a small way by delegating important (but not critically important) tasks, you will be rewarded by the satisfaction of watching people develop their skills, abilities and career prospects.

   Some managers make the mistake of withholding development opportunities from their staff. They do this because they worry that their subordinates, given half a chance, might ultimately challenge their own status and power.

**CASE STUDY**

Mike, a College Principal, explains how he was once caught in this trap:

*'When I worked as a Head of Department I was responsible for a number of staff, many of whom were very competent people. I had worked my way up to the management team in the College and, I suppose, I guarded my position quite jealously. Looking back, I think I was worried that if other people were seen to be able to do what I could do, then it would reflect badly on me. Eventually, of course, I became worn out and totally stressed, because I was trying to do everything and shoulder all the responsibility. I felt defeated by it all and, very much in the spirit of 'Oh, what the hell', I started to offload work and delegate responsibility to the people I trusted most. Nothing dreadful happened! Instead, people began to blossom — use their initiative to make improvements and develop new and exciting projects. So, suddenly I had a department that was, for the most part, running smoothly and producing really good results. That success gave me the confidence to apply for, and get, my current job.'*

## FORMAL AND STRUCTURED STAFF DEVELOPMENT

This kind of staff development involves structured training and learning opportunities for both individuals and teams.

**ACTIVITY 11**

List four kinds of structured training or learning opportunities that can be used to develop staff.

1

2

3

4

---

**FEEDBACK**

Formal, structured training and learning opportunities include:

- attending courses, seminars, lectures, workshops; reading books and watching videos
- working through an open learning or distance learning workbook or CD-ROM
- secondment to a different organization, location, function, department or section
- shadowing and/or being coached by a more experienced colleague
- involvement in a formal mentoring programme within the organization

Each of these opportunities has their own benefits and advantages and the choice should be dictated by the needs of:

- the individual
- the team
- the organization

---

# Training needs analysis (TNA)/training audit

Training Needs Analysis (TNA) and Training Audit – the terms mean the same thing, and are interchangeable – are the processes that address three key questions:

- what can this person do, at the moment, and what does this person know, at the moment?
- so that the organization can meet the standards, targets and objectives that have been set, what does this person need to be able to do, and need to know?
- what kind of training or learning opportunities would be most appropriate for this person to enable them to acquire the skills and knowledge (and, maybe, change of attitude) required?

## TOTAL TRAINING NEEDS ANALYSIS/TRAINING AUDIT

Often, Training Needs Analysis is used when an organization seeks to:

- provide staff with completely new skills or knowledge
- improve or update existing staff skills, knowledge or attitude in order to enhance current performance

The three key questions:

- what does he or she know?
- what does he or she need to know?
- what training or learning would best close the gap?

are asked in respect of each individual member of staff within the organization, no matter how senior or how junior that person might be. Because of the size and scope of this kind of project, a Total TNA is normally only undertaken when:

- a brand new company is to be created
- there is product or service diversification which requires staff to acquire a range of new knowledge and skills
- the company is seeking Investors in People accreditation
- the organization is teetering on the brink of disaster and it is felt that a major new training initiative is the only solution

## SELECTIVE TRAINING NEEDS ANALYSIS/TRAINING AUDIT

The three key questions are asked of a specific group of people, or perhaps even just one person. For example, administrative staff; first-line supervisors; everyone in the sales function; the team responsible for launching the microwave kettle; or Tom in accounts whose attitude problem has upset three suppliers this month already.

# Understanding organizational objectives

Before undertaking any kind of training needs analysis or training audit, you need to make sure that you understand the standards, targets or objectives that the organization has set for itself. For example:

- Increase market share by 10 per cent by December 1997
- Decrease computer down-time by 20 per cent by January 1998
- Improve internal communication systems by Spring 1998
- Publish Complete Works of Shakespeare on CD-ROM by March 1998
- Achieve Investors in People by May 1998

Once you are clear about organizational objectives, then you can begin to think about the skills, knowledge and attitudes the staff should possess in order to achieve the desired outcome. For example:

---

**OBJECTIVE: Improve internal communication systems by Spring 1998**

Skills needed
Ability to:

- give clear explanations and instructions
- listen
- clarify and summarize
- question
- give appropriate feedback
- write clear and concise reports
- cascade information through team briefings
- present statistics and numerical information through visual presentations
- communicate using internal e-mail

Knowledge needed

- Communication loop
- Difference between open, closed, leading and probing questions
- Interpretation of body language
- Bar and Gantt charts
- Spelling, grammar, punctuation
- Format for business correspondence
- PowerPoint software

Attitudes needed

- Co-operation and team-working
- Willingness to share information

---

The next step in the process is to find out what people currently can do and know. Once you have that information you can fill the gap with appropriate training and learning opportunities.

| Current position | Closing the Gap | Desired position |
|---|---|---|
| can't do | TRAINING AND LEARNING OPPORTUNITY | can do |
| don't know | TRAINING AND LEARNING OPPORTUNITY | do know |

**Figure 3**  Closing the gap between the current position and the desired position

## ACTIVITY 12                                                                      C10.1

How would you identify the gaps between what your staff currently know and can do and what they need to know and do?

## FEEDBACK

You can find out the information you need by using one or more of the following methods (in any combination).

### Staff interviews

This technique involves sitting down with each member of staff, asking the right kinds of questions and listening carefully to the answers. When staff training needs analysis/training audit interviews are conducted thoroughly this can often be the best (and the most time consuming), way to find out what you need to know.

### Issuing questionnaires

Providing the questionnaires are carefully designed by someone who has the right kind of expertise, they can provide a great deal of useful information. Figure 4 is a brief example of a training needs analysis questionnaire.

### Journal keeping

This process involves asking each member of staff to keep a work journal in which they record each task completed and each problem encountered. The journals are subsequently analysed to identify training needs. The main drawback with this technique is that even though people may set out with the best of intentions, journal keeping is time-consuming and requires focus and attention to detail. Important information can easily be omitted, so the journal may, in the end, prove to be a worthless document.

### Observation

Using this approach, staff are observed as they carry out specific tasks. The observer identifies the skills and knowledge used, assesses the level of performance and analyses the skills and knowledge needed. Again, this is a time-consuming and laborious technique, particularly if a large number of staff are involved.

Broadly speaking, most companies use a combination of questionnaires and interviews to identify the gaps which need to be plugged by training of one kind or another.

| NAME: |  |
|---|---|
| JOB TITLE: |  |
| DATE: |  |
| So far, what training have you received in Windows '95 software? |  |
| Is there any additional aspect of Windows '95 software training you feel you would benefit from? |  |
| How often do you use Windows '95? |  |
| For what purpose do you most often use Windows '95? |  |
| What problems do you most often encounter when using Windows '95? |  |
| When problems occur, what action do you usually take? |  |
| For you, what is the most difficult part of using Windows '95? |  |
| How useful do you find the Windows '95 instruction manual? |  |
| How often do you consult the instruction manual? |  |
| What changes or additions to the manual would be most useful to you? |  |
| Why would these changes or additions be useful? |  |

**Figure 4**    Training needs analysis questionaire

**Assessment**

Observation is an example of an assessment process, but there are other options available. Tests, simulations and case studies are often used, sometimes in the context of structured assessment centres.

Needs can also be identified through review of performance, often through structured performance management systems such as appraisal. Finally, needs can be identified through systems such as 360 degree appraisal.

Provide the information requested in the chart below, using a separate sheet of paper if you prefer, in order to ensure confidentiality.

**Note:** This activity should relate to members of your team – those people for whose development you have some measure of responsibility. Complete a separate chart for each team member.

| NAME:                                                    JOB TITLE: | | |
|---|---|---|
| Date on which I carried out Training Needs Analysis:<br><br>Methods I used to obtain the information: | | |
| Existing skills and knowledge | Proposed training intended to close the skills and knowledge gap | Required skills and knowledge |
| | | |
| | | |
| | | |
| | | |
| | | |
| | | |
| | | |

# Investors in People

Investors in People (often referred to as IiP) is a government initiative originally devised by the Employment Department – now the Department for Employment and Education. The goal of IiP is to help organizations develop their people, through training and learning opportunities, in order to achieve the organization's business objectives.

Any organization wishing to achieve Investors in People must meet four principal requirements:

1   **Public commitment from the top to develop all employees to achieve the organization's business objectives.** This means that there must be a public commitment, from the most senior people in the business, to develop all staff. This must go far beyond a token statement of intent. Genuine commitment to IiP must:

- cascade down from every senior manager
- be written into the company's strategic plan
- be supported by public notices of commitment
- be reinforced by regular meetings to encourage and support the process

2   **Regular reviews of the training and development needs of all employees.** IiP requires companies to regularly review training and development needs against business objectives, as well as regularly undertaking a review of individual staff member's training and development needs. This review may be done either through training needs analysis or performance appraisal. (Performance appraisal is dealt with in detail in Workbook 14, *The New Model Leader*.)

In addition, managers must verify that they are competent to develop other people. This may be done through their own performance appraisal, through assessment against the MCI management competences or through gaining a National Vocational Qualification (NVQ).

3   **Continuing action to train and develop individuals on recruitment and throughout their employment.** Companies hoping to gain IiP must:

- have an effective induction programme for new employees
- provide new employees with the training and development they need to do their job
- ensure that existing employees are developed in line with business objectives

Investors in People requires that all employees are made aware of the development opportunities which are open to them. These may include:

- special projects, work shadowing, job rotation, secondment
- courses, open learning, coaching, mentoring

In an organization seeking IiP accreditation, managers have a responsibility to encourage and support employees in identifying and meeting their job-related development needs.

4   **Regular evaluation of the investment in training and development to assess achievement and improve its future effectiveness.** A company seeking IiP accreditation must evaluate:

- how its development of people is contributing to business goals and targets
- whether or not the development action taken is effective

In addition to completing post-training evaluation questionnaires, organizations can evaluate training through:

- discussion at performance appraisal

- team de-briefing sessions
- meetings between individual members of staff and their line manager

As part of the IiP process, companies need to compile a portfolio which contains evidence that action is being taken to meet the four principal requirements. Because accreditation as an Investor in People is gained through a process of assessment, the organization must send a letter of intent to their local TEC or LEC (Training Enterprise Council, England & Wales/Local Enterprise Company, Scotland), or to the Training and Employment Agency (in Northern Ireland).

## ACTIVITY 14

For the purpose of this activity, assume that your Chairperson, MD or CEO has informed you that your organization is going to seek Investors in People accreditation. Your task is to create an action plan of things to do to ensure that the company meets the four principal IiP requirements. In the space below list up to fifteen actions you would take to get IiP up and running in your company.

1

2

3

4

5

6

7

8

9

10

11

12

13

14

15

## FEEDBACK

Fifteen steps that would set you firmly on the road to achieving Investors in People accreditation would be:

1 Read and absorb the IiP Standard so that you clearly understand (a) what is required, and (b) the implications for your company and its staff

2 Link the Standard and your company's Strategic Plan so that training and development are firmly on the agenda

3 Appoint an IiP Co-ordinator to co-ordinate and administer the programme. Ideally, this would be someone who has expertise in the area of training and development

4 Run a Training Needs Analysis to find out (a) where people are now, and (b) where people need to be if they are to be able to meet the company's business objectives

5 Produce an Action Plan to meet the four principal IiP requirements and have this agreed by senior management

6 Set up a Steering Group composed of people at different levels and from different functions within the company. The role of the Steering Group should be to provide help and support with the implementation of the programme, monitor progress and channel feedback

7 Make the commitment, in writing, to the appropriate TEC or LEC, once you know your organization's staff are with you

8 Communicate throughout the business and let everyone know what IiP is all about; what it means for individuals, teams and the company as a whole; let people know what is contained in the IiP Action Plan

9 Plan the Training and Development Opportunities by deciding what is going to happen, to whom, when, and the way in which the success of each opportunity is to be evaluated

10 Assign and allocate resources – finance for the training budget, space, equipment and, of course, management time

11 Gather evidence to prove that the company is meeting the IiP requirements. An assessor (from the TEC or LEC) will visit your organization to meet staff and also to examine the portfolio of evidence

12 Monitor progress on a regular basis, (at least two or three times a year), to make sure that everything is happening when it is supposed to happen, and in the way in which it's supposed to happen

13 Set up a sample assessment. Ask your IiP adviser to run a sample assessment to check how close you are to achieving the required Standard. This will enable you to make any necessary adjustments prior to the formal assessment

14 Prepare for assessment. Assessment is carried out through: (a) examination of the portfolio of evidence; (b) interviews with your staff, carried out by accredited assessors. The assessors will discuss IiP and ask questions about the four IiP principles

15 Keep going. Once your organization has been awarded IiP status it is vital to keep going, because there will be periodic assessments to ensure that your company still meets the IiP requirements

The next activity will give you an opportunity to think about the way in which staff development needs are currently identified within your organization.

**ACTIVITY 15**                                                               C10.1

Consider the following questions and note down your answers.

1   Currently, what system, method, process or technique is used within your organization to identify:
    a   individual training and development needs?


    b   team training and development needs?


2   How are individual and team training and development needs matched to corporate objectives?


3   How do you identify your own training and development needs?


4   What contribution do you personally make to the process of identifying staff training and development needs?


5   Given a free hand, what changes or improvements would you make to the systems and procedures currently used in your organization to identify and meet training and development needs?

# Summary

- Developing people is the process of enabling individuals to improve existing and acquire new:
    - skills
    - knowledge
    - attitudes
- The benefits of staff development include **reduced**:
    - down-time on plant and machinery
    - wastage and breakages
    - accidents
    - drifting schedules and failure to meet production targets
    - over-spending on budgets

    and **improved**:
    - competitive advantage
    - quality and customer service leading to increased customer satisfaction and loyalty
    - staff motivation, communication and team-working
    - labour retention
- The costs of not developing staff include:
    - financial costs: down-time, breakages, waste, disruption to production schedules and budgets, absenteeism, recruitment, loss of competitive advantage
    - reputation costs: accidents, poor quality and customer service, disputes with unions and staff organizations
    - efficiency costs: poor internal and external communication, ineffective team working, low staff motivation and morale, resistance to change, lack of innovative ideas
- Staff development can be:
    - Informal and organic – offering people development opportunities as and when those opportunities arise
    - formal and structured – a planned programme offering structured training and learning opportunities to individuals and teams
- Training needs analysis/training audit are the processes which address three key questions:
    a   what can this person do at the moment, and what does this person know at the moment?
    b   so that the organization can meet the standards, targets and objectives which have been set, what does this person need to be able to do and need to know?

   c   what kind of training or learning opportunities would be most appropriate for this person to help them to close the gap between can't do & can do, and don't know & do know?

- An analysis of staff training needs can be undertaken through:
  - interviews
  - questionnaires
  - journals
  - observation

- The four principal requirements of the Investors in People programme are:
  - Public commitment from the top to develop all employees to achieve the organization's business objectives
  - Regular reviews of the training and development needs of all employees
  - Continuing action to train and develop individuals on recruitment and throughout their employment
  - Regular evaluation of the investment in training and development to assess achievement and improve its future effectiveness

- The steps that will set you on the road to Investors in People accreditation are:
  1. Make sure you understand the IiP Standard
  2. Link the Standard and your company's Strategic Plan
  3. Appoint an IiP Co-ordinator
  4. Carry out a Training Needs Analysis
  5. Produce an Action Plan
  6. Set up a Steering Group
  7. Inform your TEC or LEC
  8. Communicate about IiP to everyone in the organization
  9. Plan the training and development opportunities
  10. Assign and allocate resources
  11. Gather evidence to prove that organization is meeting the IiP Standard
  12. Monitor progress
  13. Set up a sample assessment and request a visit from your TEC or LEC assessor
  14. Prepare for assessment
  15. Keep going (even if the going gets tough!)

# Section 4 Planning and running training sessions

## Introduction

Within the best organizations – those which have made a serious commitment to staff development – training is not solely the responsibility of the training department. Everyone in the organization, from the top down, takes responsibility for making sure that staff development needs are met through the most effective and most relevant training and learning opportunities.

In this section of the workbook we are focusing on the design and delivery of effective training so that you will be in a better position to either prepare and run a training session, or assess and evaluate the effectiveness of training within your organization.

For the sake of clarity and simplicity, in this section, the words 'trainer' and 'facilitator' are interchangeable, and mean the same thing. Here, these words are used to describe someone who presents information about any topic or skill, to a group of people, in the hope that **learning** will take place.

## Are you working in a 'learning organization?'

Some businesses trust to luck and hope that staff keep their heads down, get on with the job and find out what they need to know, when they need to know it. Fortunately many businesses have now moved on from this position and can now can be described as a 'learning organization'. This definition was coined by Alan Mumford in the book *Management Development: Strategies for Action*[1]. Learning organizations actively encourage and support staff development and training, using a wide range of approaches and techniques. Some of these may be categorized as formal training interventions, and some may be informal development opportunities which are routinely presented and which spring from, and contribute towards, the culture of the company.

## ACTIVITY 16

List five different informal staff development opportunities which might be available to you, as an employee of a business that could be described as a learning organization.

1

2

3

4

5

## FEEDBACK

If your company is a learning organization then, at work, you will be provided with:

- encouragement to identify your own learning needs
- reviews on your ability to develop your staff
- regular reviews of your performance
- constructive feedback on your performance
- opportunities to set challenging learning goals for yourself
- assistance with helping you to see learning opportunities on the job
- new experiences that will provide you with new learning opportunities
- leeway to make some mistakes, providing you learn from them
- encouragement to challenge the traditional ways of doing things[2]

In addition, you will also have structured learning opportunities – such as courses, seminars and workshops – specifically designed to close any gaps in your skills or knowledge.

# Closing the gaps

When we learn we acquire new skills, knowledge or attitudes through the process of:

- experiencing (doing, hearing or reading about something)
- reflecting (thinking about what we have done, heard or read)
- forming abstract concepts and generalizations (drawing conclusions from our reflections)
- testing concepts in new situations (trying different things)

Figure 5 shows the loop that this process creates.

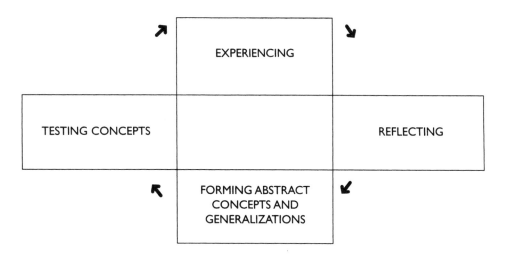

**Figure 5**   Kolb's learning cycle

In practice, the process works like this.

1   You decide to send an e-mail using your newly installed e-mail sending software programme. You do everything you are supposed to (you think), and proudly click the 'send' button. With a relieved sigh and a little smile of satisfaction you go about your business. (This is the experience.)

2   Later in the day you return to the e-mail software and discover, to your disappointment, that your carefully composed message has been returned to you with a curt on-screen note saying 'Unable to deliver – host address unknown.' You read the instruction book and check that you did everything right; you ask a colleague for their opinion and discuss what you did; you scratch your head and think hard about what might have gone wrong. (This is the reflecting part of the process.)

3   You decide, in the light of all the available information, that the problem occurred because you omitted the word 'INTERNET' at the start of the recipient's address. (You are forming abstract concepts and generalizations.)

4   You change the recipient's address to include the word 'INTERNET' and, holding your breath and hoping that it works, you click the 'send' button again. (You are testing concepts.)

At this point, anything can happen. If the recipient receives the e-mail then you will have **learned** to include the word INTERNET in the address. If – even with this change – the e-mail is returned to you, you will have to go through the whole process again, and again, and maybe even again to **learn** what it is you need to do.

Eventually, once you have got the hang of it, you will become so familiar with the process of creating and sending e-mail that you no longer have to consult the manual, or even really think about what you are doing. You will have learned something new and there will be a relatively permanent change in behaviour that occurs as a result of practice or experience.[3]

Regardless of whether you are:

- personally responsible for some aspect of the design and delivery of training
- responsible for managing the delivery of training opportunities presented by training specialists or external consultants
- required to undertake some staff development as part of your managerial role

it is important for you to understand the learning cycle. You also need a working knowledge of the factors involved in designing and delivering effective training and learning opportunities, and you should appreciate that different people learn in different ways, and at different speeds. Learning a new skill (say, using a multi-feature photocopier) may be difficult for you, and easy for John. Understanding, say, the difference between the accounting terms Internal Rate of Return and Net Present Value may be easy for you, and difficult for John. Generally, say, you may learn more slowly than John; John may need hands-on, experiential learning, whereas you may benefit most from reflective study, working alone.

## ACTIVITY 50

In the chart below you will find a list of factors which an effective trainer will provide in order to make a training and learning opportunity (say a workshop or course) a useful and relevant experience. Your task is to rank these factors in order of importance – the most important to be ranked as 1, and the least important to be ranked as 7.

| Factor | Importance |
|---|---|
| Learning objectives should be set so that learners understand what they should be able to know and do when they have completed the training. | |
| Learners should receive feedback and guidance as they learn so they can judge their progress. | |
| Learners should enjoy the learning process and feel that the learning is both useful and relevant to them and their needs. | |
| Learners should be actively involved in the learning process. | |
| Learners' interest should be aroused through the use of a variety of training techniques. | |
| Learners should be given time to practise and absorb new skills and information. | |
| Allowances should be made for individual learning styles and learning speeds. | |

## FEEDBACK

Ideally you will have identified that each of these factors are co-dependent on the others, and all are equally as important. For example, it would be pointless to run a training session packed with varied training activities if, from the point of view of the learners, the training content was meaningless and irrelevant to them. It would be pointless to make allowances for individual learning styles and speeds if the training was incomprehensible or boring and the learners were frustrated, irritated and longing to get away from the workshop.

| Variety | Learning objectives | Opportunities to learn according to their own style and speed |
|---------|--------------------|----------------------------|
| Involvement | **LEARNERS NEED** | Feedback and guidance |
| Time to absorb new information | Relevant content | Time to practise new skills |

**Figure 6**   The factors that help learners to learn

The secret of designing effective training and learning opportunities lies in building each of these factors in to the training event, in equal proportion.

## LEARNING OBJECTIVES

Learning objectives are statements that clearly explain what learners will know or be able to do when they have completed the training. The three main purposes of learning objectives are that they:

- give the training designer a structure and framework upon which to build a training event
- let the learners know what to expect from the training
- enable everyone involved – trainers, learners, interested managers – to evaluate whether or not the training has been successful and achieved the learning objectives

Learning objectives should be easy to understand and should state, clearly and concisely, what learners should be able to do when they have completed the training. For example:

- design a critical path analysis chart
- demonstrate three different techniques for closing a sale
- explain the difference between variable and fixed costs
- describe the benefits of National Vocational Qualifications
- prepare a report describing the benefits of experiential learning
- analyse our regional sales statistics for 1996/97

When creating learning objectives, avoid words such 'know' and 'understand', for example:

- know how to listen effectively
- understand the difference between profit and loss

'Know' and 'understand' as learning objectives are difficult to measure. What does someone have to do to show they know or understand something? If outcomes are hard to measure then it follows that success or failure will be difficult to evaluate.

## ACTIVITY 18

For the purpose of this activity imagine that it has been decided that everyone in the management team in your organization would benefit from a course in Communication Skills. The aim of the course is to ensure that, after the training, managers will be able to use clear verbal communication.

Your task is to prepare a list of five learning objectives which will:

a  help the trainer to design the course
b  tell the participants what they will be able to do and know after the training
c  provide a benchmark for success against which the learning can be measured

At the end of the course participants will be able to:

1
2
3
4
5

## FEEDBACK

Your list of learning objectives may include some of the following:

- Give clear instructions
- Explain complex information in a clear and straightforward manner
- Answer questions thoroughly
- Demonstrate effective listening skills
- Use active listening skills
- Use a range of questioning techniques
- Ask appropriate questions to discover relevant information
- Summarize the content of a conversation
- Explain the difference between 'open' and 'closed' questions
- Describe five characteristics of effective verbal communication

Once the learning objectives have been decided, then the person who is designing the training event can decide what information and practical exercises should be included so that learners will be able to achieve the desired outcomes.

## VARIETY AND INVOLVEMENT

Anyone who has sat on a hard chair in a stuffy, overheated room listening to six hours of unadulterated 'chalk and talk' knows only too well that learning something new can be an excruciatingly boring and demoralizing experience.

Equally, given an interested and interesting presenter together with a range of varied learning exercises, learning can be an enjoyable and stimulating activity.

The average attention span of most people (no matter how motivated or intelligent they might be) is between ten and twenty minutes, maximum. After that, people 'switch off'. Not necessarily because they want to switch off, but because that is the maximum amount of time people can give to absorbing new information. In practice, this means that a trainer who gives a chalk and talk lecture for longer than twenty minutes is wasting everyone's time.

People learn best through **experiential learning**. That is, learning in which they participate and are actively involved. Exercises which allow people to generate and share ideas, work together as a team or carry out practical tasks help learners to learn.

## ACTIVITY 19

Reflect back on the most interesting, challenging, enjoyable and informative training in which you have been involved as a learner. Note down, in the space below, four different training techniques or activities which were used by the trainer to provide variety and involvement for the participants on the course.

1

2

3

4

## FEEDBACK

You may have experienced some, or all, of the following techniques:

- Working as a member of a team, in competition with another team
- Working as a member of a small syndicate of perhaps three or four people
- Working in a trio where two people practise a skill, and the third person observes and comments
- Working as one half of a partnership
- Working as an individual, in competition with everyone else in the learning group

You may have participated in one or more of the following activities:

- brainstorming – where everyone's contribution, no matter how outrageous or apparently irrelevant, is cheerfully accepted and, possibly, used to spark additional, creative ideas from others in the group
- creation of lists of ideas in response to specific questions asked by the group's trainer or facilitator
- group discussion
- research and presentation of information
- practice/demonstration of a skill
- problem solving – perhaps using case studies

No matter what the topic or who the learners are (whether junior shopfloor staff or members of the Board), providing training that is varied, and which requires learner involvement, is the key to success.

## RELEVANT CONTENT

Training should be relevant and pitched at an appropriate level for the learners. For instance, participants who have been booked onto a health and safety course do not want to know about the history of trade unionism; learners looking forward to updating their time management skills do not want a detailed explanation of Critical Path Analysis, and the senior management team, keen to improve internal communications, do not want to know which system is currently used to allocate spaces in the staff car park.

Learners need to feel that the content of the training (the information being presented) and the practical exercises and activities in which they are participating:

- are current and up to date
- are useful and practical
- will help them to be more efficient and effective
- can be used by them in their work
- may contribute, in a positive way, to their career prospects

## FEEDBACK AND GUIDANCE

Everyone, from the CEO down, needs to know how they are doing. Getting the answers to questions like:

- Am I doing OK?
- Am I doing as well as – or better than – my colleagues?
- Am I meeting other people's expectations?

is particularly important when people are involved in acquiring new knowledge or learning new skills.

Learners who do not receive constructive feedback and helpful guidance in a training situation may quickly become disenchanted, and can think:

- This trainer doesn't care how I'm doing – so the course can't be that important.
- I'm not getting any feedback – I must be doing really badly – so there's no point in trying ... I'll just give up now.
- This trainer doesn't like me – so why should I like them?
- Does this trainer know what they're doing?

Acknowledging learners' efforts and providing encouragement and support are key parts of the trainer's or facilitator's role.

## DIFFERENT KINDS OF LEARNING OPPORTUNITY

As you saw from Activity 5 (p. 12), different people prefer to learn in different ways. A well-designed course, seminar or workshop will take account of these differences, and will provide a range of different learning opportunities to suit everyone. For example:

- hands-on exercises to help the Activists to learn
- demonstrations and practical examples to help the Reflectors to learn
- clear, logical explanations to help the Theorists to learn
- discussion and real-life examples of how the training topic can be applied in a practical way at work, to help the Pragmatists to learn

## TIME TO ABSORB INFORMATION AND PRACTISE NEW SKILLS

Correct pacing is vital to the success of a training course, workshop or seminar. 'Pacing' is really about the speed at which new topics are introduced, and the amount of time given to each. Courses that are too slow spend far too long on one discussion or one activity, so that participants get bored and restless and begin to wish they were back at work, doing something useful. Courses that are too fast rush, helter-skelter, from one topic to another, nothing is covered in depth, no one has time to consider the information, and everyone leaves the training none the wiser for the experience.

Effective trainers and facilitators provide opportunities for people to reflect on what has been learned and to think about how they can apply the principles, in practice, to real-life situations. They do this through:

- discussions
- question and answer sessions
- providing relevant case studies and examples which demonstrate how the principle works in practice
- allowing frequent breaks which give learners the opportunity to process and absorb new information

# Planning a training event

From time to time you may, as a manager, be required to plan a training session. Or, you may have to assess and evaluate the way a training session has been designed and delivered by an external consultant, or someone from your own organization's training function.

An effective training on any topic will address the key questions:

■ what do they know, and what can they do?
■ what do they need to know, and need to do?

## IDENTIFY THE GAPS AND WRITE THE LEARNING OBJECTIVES

When planning a training session your first step is to identify the gap, and then write the learning objectives, for example:

*By the end of the session learners will be able to:*

■ *write clear and concise business reports*
■ *present numerical data in an easy to understand, graphical format*
■ *prepare a range of standard format business letters*

## KNOWLEDGE CONTENT

Once you have written the learning objectives, your next step is to think about the knowledge the learners will need in order to achieve the desired outcomes, for example:

*Write clear and concise business reports – knowledge:*

■ Use double spacing on A4 paper
■ Keep sentences short
■ Divide information into sections and label each clearly with a different heading

This is the **theory** part of the course, and this information is usually delivered by the trainer using a variety of techniques including:

■ overhead projector acetates
■ flipcharts
■ paper-based information, which is handed out
■ question and answer session

## PRACTICAL CONTENT

Your next step is to consider what kind of **practical** learning activities you can provide for the learners so that they can become actively involved, for example:

*Write clear and concise business reports – activities:*

■ *In pairs, read through this report, comment on its clarity and suggest ways in which it might be improved*

- *In teams, prepare a one-page report on 'Where our company will be five years from now'*
- *As a group, brainstorm the key elements of a clear and concise business report*

## PLANNING THE TIME

Once you know the:

- theory you will be presenting to the group
- type and number of activities you will be asking the group to participate in

your next task is to work out a rough timetable for the session. An example training session timetable is shown in Figure 7.

| Morning 9.30am–1pm | Afternoon 2pm–5.30pm |
|---|---|
| 9.30–10.00 Group introductions | 2.00–2.15 Trainer input – re-cap on main learning points from this morning |
| 10.00–10.30 Group brainstorm – key points of a good report | 2.15–3.30 Team activity: two teams in competition – preparing a one-page report on 'Where our business will be five years from now' |
| 10.30–10.45 Discussion | 3.30–3.45 Feedback and discussion |
| 10.45–11.15 Coffee | 3.45–4.00 Coffee |
| 11.15–11.45 Trainer input and presentation of theory – OHP acetates | 4.00–4.45 Individual activity: write a one-page report on 'The key learning points from this course' |
| 11.45–12.30 Pairs activity – comments and suggestions on a business report – samples provided | 4.45–5.30 Presentation and discussion of the reports |
| 12.30–1.00 Feedback and discussion<br><br>1.00 Lunch | 5.30 Participants complete course evaluation reports; trainer closes the course |

**Figure 7**   Timetable for one-day session on writing business reports

## PLANNING THE RESOURCES

As anyone who has ever delivered a training session knows only too well, having the right amount of the right kind of resources will make the difference between a smooth-running, enjoyable event and one that is chaotic and irritating for everyone concerned.

## ACTIVITY 20

Consider the timetable shown in Figure 7, and complete the chart below by noting the resources you would need if you were planning to deliver this training session to a group of fourteen people.

| Activity | Resources needed |
|---|---|
| 9.30–10.00 Group introductions | |
| 10.00–10.30 Group brainstorm – key points of a good report | |
| 10.30–10.45 Discussion | |
| 11.15–11.45 Trainer input and presentation of theory – OHP acetates | |
| 11.45–12.30 Pairs activity – comments and suggestions on a business report – samples provided | |
| 12.30–1.00 Feedback and discussion | |
| 2.00–2.15 Trainer input – re-cap on main learning points from this morning | |
| 2.15–3.30 Team activity: two teams in competition – preparing a one-page report on 'Where our business will be five years from now' | |
| 3.30–3.45 Feedback and discussion | |
| 4.00–4.45 Individual activity: write a one-page report on 'The key learning points from this course' | |
| 4.45–5.30 Presentation and discussion of the reports | |
| 5.30 Participants complete course evaluation reports; trainer closes the course | |

## FEEDBACK

Ideally, your completed chart should look something like this:

| Activity | Resources needed |
|---|---|
| 9.30–10.00 Group introductions | ■ Name cards for trainer and participants<br>■ Overhead Projector<br>■ Spare bulb for OHP<br>■ OHP acetate showing learning objectives for the course |
| 10.00–10.30 Group brainstorm – key points of a good report | ■ flipcharts and easels<br>■ marker pens<br>■ scrap paper<br>■ biros, pencils<br>■ Blu-Tak |
| 11.15–11.45 Trainer input and presentation of theory – OHP acetates | ■ OHP acetates<br>■ Key Points and notes to be handed out × 14 sets |
| 11.45–12.30 Pairs activity – comments and suggestions on a business report – samples provided | ■ sample reports to be handed out to pairs × 7<br>■ flipcharts<br>■ marker pens<br>■ Blu-Tak |
| 2.15–3.30 Team activity: two teams in competition – preparing a one-page report on 'Where our business will be five years from now' | ■ scrap paper<br>■ biros and pencils<br>■ dictionary × 2<br>■ thesaurus × 2 |
| 4.00–4.45 Individual activity: write a one-page report on 'The key learning points from this course' | ■ scrap paper<br>■ biros and pencils<br>■ dictionary<br>■ thesaurus<br>■ 3 × 5 record cards × 100 |
| 4.45–5.30 Presentation and discussion of the reports | ■ flipcharts<br>■ marker pens<br>■ Blu-Tak |
| 5.30 Participants complete course evaluation reports; trainer closes the course | ■ Key Points and notes to be handed out × 14 sets<br>course evaluation reports × 14 |

## PREPARING THE RESOURCES

The next step is to prepare the resources you will need for the session. This may involve:

■ creating overhead projector acetates, which can be done by hand or by using a specialist presentation computer software program such as, for example, PowerPoint, Freelance or PageMaker. Used in conjunction with a trainer's words, acetates showing key learning points, pictures or graphs reinforce what is being said and help learners to remember the information. Acetates:

- explain, amplify or clarify points
- hold attention, help concentration and aid retention
- add interest and variety
- writing the handouts, which are usually best produced on a word-processor and then photocopied. Handouts should be:
    - straightforward, easy to understand, jargon-free
    - clear and easy to read
    - contain relevant information and key learning points
- gathering together the flipcharts and pads, pens, evaluation sheets and any other equipment, stationery, tools or props you intend to use

## PREPARING THE TRAINING ROOM

The training room should be:

- well lit (preferably by daylight) and well ventilated
- heated or cooled to an appropriate temperature
- sufficiently large to contain, comfortably, all the participants, the trainer and the equipment
- provide the right number of comfortable chairs and tables
- clean and tidy

These are important factors and every care and attention should be paid to the comfort and well-being of the participants. Unhappy, uncomfortable people who are too hot, too cold or overcrowded will not and cannot concentrate and focus on anything other than how hot, or cold, or crowded or uncomfortable they are. For the sake of the participants, and in the cause of self-preservation, trainers should not ignore these basic needs.

## DELIVERING THE TRAINING

You have designed the course, prepared the resources, booked the room and informed the delegates that you will be expecting them to arrive on a particular day at a specific time. All that's left to do is facilitate the event itself.

## ACTIVITY 21

Cast your mind back over the training events which you have attended, in the past, as a participant. Think about the qualities and skills needed by an effective facilitator, and also some of the qualities and skills you may have seen demonstrated by an ineffective facilitator. Then complete the chart below.

| Skills and qualities of an effective facilitator | Skills and qualities of an ineffective facilitator |
|---|---|
| 1 | 1 |
| 2 | 2 |
| 3 | 3 |
| 4 | 4 |
| 5 | 5 |
| 6 | 6 |

## FEEDBACK

**Effective** training facilitators:

- are comfortable with and knowledgeable about the topic they are presenting
- make sure they are well prepared and well rehearsed
- welcome the participants and put people at their ease
- agree the ground rules with the group – breaks, smoking, timing, etc.
- start the session with an appropriate exercise to 'break the ice' and settle the participants into a learning frame of mind
- use equipment – overhead projector, flipchart, video, etc. – confidently and competently
- speak clearly, write legibly
- invite questions and answer them carefully and intelligently
- involve everyone – even those who have 'done this before'; 'haven't got time for this'; 'can't see the point'; or 'know it won't work in practice'
- respect the participants – they recognize they are dealing with adults, and they behave accordingly
- pay equal attention to all contributions
- watch for signs of boredom or stress – and take appropriate action by adjusting the pace, or varying the activities

- remain even tempered and good humoured (under all circumstances)
- offer useful and constructive feedback, guidance and advice
- adapt the session (if necessary) to meet the needs of the group

**Effective** training facilitators:

- don't ignore the mood or needs of the group and simply soldier on, regardless
- don't pay attention only to the brightest or the most amenable participants
- don't use inappropriate humour to make jokes at the expense of participants
- are not sarcastic, bullying, critical, judgemental, condescending and/or patronizing
- don't waste time and/or go over time
- don't talk incessantly
- don't refuse to answer questions
- don't assume that if the participants don't understand, it's the participants' fault, and nothing to do with the facilitator
- don't allow the strongest personalities in the group to take over
- don't allow their own boredom, tiredness or irritation to shine out like a beacon to everyone in the room
- don't pretend they 'know it all', when they don't

# Evaluating training

Evaluation is the process of analysing the value of something. Sound evaluation of any training intervention (e.g. course, workshop, seminar, open/distance learning programme, etc.) is equally important for:

- individual participants
- the training function
- the business

## ACTIVITY 22

What are the benefits of evaluating the success or failure of training?

List two benefits of evaluation for the individual participant:

1

2

List two benefits of evaluation for the training function:

1

2

List two benefits of evaluation for the business as a whole:

1

2

## FEEDBACK

**Benefits of evaluation for individual participants:**

Learners can:

- safely, and without fear of reprisal, give their honest opinion on all aspects of the training intervention, e.g. the facilities, the trainer, the content of the course, the level of participation, whether or not they achieved the outcomes stated in the learning objectives
- give feedback as to whether or not there is likely to be a change or improvement in their knowledge, level of skill or attitude, as a result of the training
- indicate whether or not different or additional, similar, training might be of value in the future

**Benefits of evaluation for the training function**

Trainers (and training managers) can:

- assess individual competence, e.g. a trainer's ability to:
    - design and prepare a training session
    - deliver a training session
    - enable learners to acquire a relatively permanent change in behaviour that occurs as a result of practice or experience
- identify success, and repeat successful training interventions
- identify failure and make appropriate changes to future sessions
- identify likely training needs for the future

**Benefits of evaluation for the business**

Organizations can:

- see where the company is in terms of staff development as it relates to the business' objectives and long-term strategic plan
- use evaluation as a basis for planning future staff development needs
- progress towards the achievement of the Investors in People Standard, (as evaluation is a key IiP requirement)
- gain relevant feedback on the effectiveness of the training function

# HOW TO EVALUATE?

## Happy sheets

At the conclusion of most training events, participants are asked to complete a Course Evaluation Form, often referred to as a Happy Sheet. An example is given in Figure 8.

Some Course Evaluation Sheets have space for the participant's name and job title, although others do not ask for this information – on the basis that guaranteed anonymity is more likely to produce honest feedback from learners.

# DE-BRIEFING SESSIONS

Following on from a training event, many companies hold a de-briefing session at which the participants are invited to discuss all aspects of the training. A key feature of many of these meetings is not only to ask 'How did it go?' but also to find out 'What would you like next?'

Training evaluation, to be meaningful, should really be carried out:

- immediately after the event – as timely feedback can signpost changes which need to be made for future sessions, and
- three to six months after the event – to check whether or not the training has actually been taken on board by the participants and has affected their knowledge, skills and ability. Training that doesn't stick, and which doesn't result in a relatively permanent change in behaviour is, at best, not good value for money and, at worst, a complete waste of time and energy.

| Programme: |
| --- |
| Date: Venue: |
| Facilitator: |
| 1  What were your expectations of this course? |
| 2  Do you feel they were met? Please say why. <br><br> If your expectations were not met, please say why. |
| 3  What did you think about: <br> ■ Programme content? <br><br> ■ Pace? <br><br> ■ Participation? <br><br> ■ Relevance to your job and your needs? |
| 4  Please rate how helpful and informative you found this training on the following scale: <br> Unhelpful                                                                                                          Very helpful <br> 1 ☐            2 ☐            3 ☐            4 ☐            5 ☐ |
| 5  Please give your reasons for your answer to question 4. |
| 6  What did you think about: <br> ■ the training facilities (room, etc.)? <br><br> ■ the food? <br><br> ■ the length of the course? |
| 7  Do you have any additional comments about any aspect of this training event? |

**Figure 8**   Sample course evaluation sheet

**ACTIVITY 23**                                                    C10.5, C10.6

1 What systems, processes and procedures are currently used, in your organization, to evaluate training?

2 How successful are these systems, processes and procedures in practice?

Highly successful          ❑
Reasonably successful      ❑
Not at all successful      ❑

Please give your reasons for your selected response:

3 What changes or improvements would you make to improve the effectiveness of current training evaluation systems, processes and procedures?

## Summary

- Companies that are learning organizations provide their people with the opportunity to:
    - identify their own learning needs
    - regularly review performance
    - set challenging learning goals
    - receive timely feedback on performance and achievement
    - review their ability to develop their staff
    - receive assistance with spotting on-the-job learning opportunities
    - access new experiences which provide new learning opportunities
    - make some mistakes – providing the mistakes are used as a learning tool
    - challenge the traditional ways of doing things
- People learn through the process (often referred to as Kolb's learning cycle) of:
    - experiencing – doing, hearing or reading about something
    - reflecting – thinking about what has been done, heard or read
    - forming abstract concepts and generalizations – drawing conclusions as a result of reflecting

- testing concepts in new situations – trying things out, doing things differently, trying to get things to work
- The key factors that enable learners to learn are:
    - learning objectives
    - relevant content
    - opportunities to learn which suit their own style and speed
    - feedback and guidance
    - time to practise new skills and absorb new information
    - varied teaching and learning techniques
    - involvement in the learning process (active rather than passive)
- Learning objectives should be:
    - easy to understand
    - measurable
    - a clear and concise statement of what the learner should be able to do when they have completed the training
- Words to avoid when writing learning objectives:
    - know
    - understand
- Examples of words to use when writing learning objectives:
    - design
    - create
    - prepare
    - list
    - describe
    - identify
    - analyse
    - produce
    - explain
    - use
    - research
- Planning a training event involves:
    - identifying the gaps between know/don't know and can do/can't do
    - writing appropriate learning objectives
    - identifying the knowledge content of the session (theory)
    - identifying the practical content of the session (exercises and activities)
    - planning the time
    - planning the resources
    - preparing the resources
    - preparing the training room
    - delivering the training
    - evaluating the training

- Effective trainers and facilitators:
  - have in-depth knowledge of the topic they are presenting – they know their stuff
  - use equipment and resources competently
  - speak clearly and write legibly
  - put learners at their ease
  - invite questions and answer them thoroughly
  - offer constructive feedback, guidance and advice
  - involve everyone and pay equal attention to everyone
  - respect the participants
  - remain calm, cheerful and even tempered throughout
  - adapt the session to meet the needs of the participants
- Ineffective and unprofessional trainers and facilitators:
  - ignore the needs of the group
  - pay attention to some participants and ignore others
  - use inappropriate humour
  - are sarcastic, bullying, critical, judgemental, condescending, patronizing
  - waste time and/or go over time
  - talk incessantly
  - are unable to answer questions
  - take the view that what they are doing is adequate, and if people don't understand it is not the facilitator's fault
  - allow the strongest, most talkative participants to take over
  - show their boredom, tiredness or irritation
  - pretend that they know it all
- Organizations can evaluate the effectiveness of training events by:
  - asking participants to complete Course Evaluation Sheets (often referred to as Happy Sheets)
  - de-briefing sessions:
    - a   immediately after the event
    - b   three to six months after the event

# Notes

1 Institute of Personnel Management (1989).

2 Adapted from *A Handbook of Personnel Management Practice* by Michael Armstrong, 4th ed, Kogan page (1994) (p. 458).

3 Bass and Vaughan (1967).

# Section 5 Coaching

## Introduction

The main aim of coaching is to develop people's work performance by taking every opportunity to:

- delegate work (especially if, for the person to whom it is delegated, it is complex, new, different, challenging, important)
- increase the level of responsibility that someone assumes
- providing the right environment and conditions in which someone can learn and practise new skills, knowledge and attitudes

All of these activities are key management tasks which will enable you to develop your team so that they improve their job performance and make a more valuable contribution to the team and the organization. This, in turn, will enable you to focus in a more concentrated way on your own objectives and special projects because, as people develop, you will feel more confident about delegating increasingly complex and important tasks.

In this section of the workbook we'll looking at the ways in which you can develop and improve your coaching skills in order to get the best from your staff.

## What does coaching mean to you?

Perhaps, as a manager, you already undertake a fair amount of coaching as part and parcel of your everyday working life. Or, maybe, you feel that coaching others is an intrusion on your time and best left to the 'experts'.

Use the following activity as an opportunity to reflect on your views about coaching.

---

**ACTIVITY 24**

Consider the statements below and choose the statement most accurately reflecting your views.

1  If someone can't do the job to the required standard, then it's their responsibility to make sure they improve ❏

Every manager has a responsibility for staff development ❏

2  Busy managers simply don't have time to coach staff ❏

Coaching is so important that it has to be a priority for managers ❏

3  Coaching can be used to help someone to develop any kind of knowledge, skill or attitude ❏

Coaching is really only useful for teaching straightforward skills ❏

4  The best way to develop staff is to make sure that they have formal training opportunities, delivered by training experts ❏

Increased responsibility, more complex tasks, reviews, special projects, discussions, briefings, feedback sessions are the most effective techniques for developing staff ❏

5  An effective coach spends most time watching and listening ❏

An effective coach spends most time telling and showing ❏

6  Learning is an organic process – it just happens ❏

Coaching is a necessary part of the learning process ❏

---

**FEEDBACK**

1  **Every manager has a responsibility for staff development.** Taking responsibility for developing the people on the team comes with the territory. Successful managers pay attention to enhancing their staff's skills and abilities, because they know that, ultimately, they will reap the rewards of developing their people, e.g. improved productivity, higher levels of motivation, increased creativity and innovation, and so on.

2  **Coaching is so important that it has to be a priority for managers.** It is certainly true that some people, when left to their own devices, will create their own development

opportunities. Most people, though, need encouragement, support, advice, guidance and constructive criticism to help them see how they could improve their job performance. Staff development, by and large, doesn't just happen. Managers have to take the lead and help it to happen.

3   **Coaching can be used to help someone develop any kind of knowledge, skill or attitude.** People can:

- acquire knowledge through discussion, and through being directed to read the appropriate books, journals or reports
- acquire skills by watching a skilled person perform a task
- acquire attitudes by having those attitudes 'modelled' for them – 'this is how I do it, now you copy me'

4   **Increased responsibility, more complex tasks, reviews, special projects, discussions, briefings, feedback sessions are the most effective techniques for developing staff.** Whilst formal training interventions are a key aspect of staff development, most people learn best on the job, in real life situations, where what they say and do really matters.

5   **An effective coach spends most time watching and listening.** Whilst people need support, encouragement and practical advice, coaching is not about constantly jumping in and taking over the job – unless, of course, you see a disaster just waiting to happen. Remember that one of the key aspects of a learning organization is allowing people to make genuine mistakes, providing they are prepared to learn from them.

6   **Coaching is a necessary part of the learning process.** Everyone needs a role model, and everyone needs to know:

- how to do something
- whether or not they are doing it 'right'
- what they could do to 'do it better'

People don't learn in isolation. They learn through experience, through modelling the way other people deal with the experience, through trying things in a different way, and through receiving appropriate and useful feedback on their performance.

# Setting coaching targets

As the result of observing someone going about their job, or as the outcome of a performance appraisal you, as a manager, may have to set specific coaching targets for certain members of staff. For example, you might think to yourself:

- 'I'll have to do something about Joanna's filing'
- 'If Tom's presentations don't improve we'll all be in hospital with terminal boredom'
- 'Mike's going to have to manage his time better'
- 'Louise will have to learn to speak up when she's on the 'phone'

In order to achieve a specific improvement, you need to set a specific target, which is Simple, Measurable, Achievable and Realistic. For example:

- 'I'll have to do something about Joanna's filing – I want her to store items numerically and cross reference them with alphabetical index cards'
- 'If Tom's presentations don't improve we'll all be in hospital with terminal boredom – I want him to present information concisely, and in a logical order; speak clearly and calmly; avoid the use of jargon; keep to an arranged time limit'
- 'Mike's going to have to manage his time better – I want him to make a minimum of twenty-five sales calls every week'
- 'Louise will have to learn to speak up when she's on the 'phone – I want her to speak clearly, without shouting, so that customers can hear what she is saying and don't have to ask her to repeat everything'

Once you know what it is you want people to do, then you can give some thought to the coaching technique that will be most effective and most likely to produce the desired results.

## ACTIVITY 25

Think back to the coaching you have received during the course of your own career. List three different activities you could use, as a manager, to coach members of staff to enable them to learn new skills, attitudes or knowledge.

1

2

3

## FEEDBACK

There are a number of different coaching techniques which can be used in a variety of different situations, with different people:

- **self-directed learning** – asking the learner to research specific information and feed this back to you
- **observation of a demonstration** – asking the learner to observe someone who is modelling expert skills (either yourself or someone else)

- **discussion** – discussing, with the learner, through question and answer and 'general conversation' the skills, knowledge or attitudes you want the learner to acquire
- **specific tasks/special projects** – asking the learner to complete a specific task or special project which involves using particular skills, attitudes or information
- **role-playing specific scenarios** – role-playing, with the learner, a specific scenario, e.g. 'OK, I'm going to negotiate for a 20 per cent discount – show me how you'd handle it', and then reviewing and discussing what happened
- **team/group discussions** – setting up a team meeting to discuss a specific issue with you acting as Chair and tutor, providing constructive comments and feedback on the group's input and suggestions
- **work shadowing** – arranging for the learner to work alongside or observe a more experienced member of staff (either yourself or someone else)
- **special opportunities** – these may include:
    - championing someone so they can attend a special training course
    - putting someone forward for a prestige project team
    - giving someone a chance to attend a special company social event
    - allowing people to meet important suppliers, subcontractors and customers

## CASE STUDY

It's important to use a range of different coaching techniques as Anna, an NHS Trust Manager, explains:

*'In a previous job my line manager used to think that coaching was simply a matter of giving me a report to read. "Read that, Anna," he used to say, "and then we'll talk about it some time." Well, I soon got wise to that. I didn't read the reports, and he never suggested we discuss them. Fortunately for me, there was a manager in the organization who spotted that I was ambitious and keen to get on. She gave me many opportunities to learn and her coaching took many different forms – she would include me in meetings and special projects, give me complex tasks and assignments, often throw me in at the deep end. But she always took the time to review what I'd done, and to make suggestions for improvement. And no matter what happened, she always supported me – even when I made a real mess of something. She took responsibility for helping me to learn – and that meant a great deal to me.'*

# Helping learners to learn

When you have your 'Coach's Hat' on, the main skills you will need to use are:

**Communication** – listening, summarizing, explaining, questioning, using appropriate body language, interpreting body language. These communication skills are covered in detail in Workbook 16, *Communication*.

**Transfer of knowledge and skills** – through explanations, demonstrations, modelling, discussions and de-briefing

**Encouragement and support** – through providing positive and useful feedback, praise, recognition of effort and achievement

**Review of progress and planning for the future** – through discussion of what has been achieved and what still needs to be achieved, and identification of future learning opportunities

## ACTIVITY 26

Read through the brief case studies that follow and then tick the box which most accurately reflects your chosen response, giving the reason for your response.

*Case study 1*

Gerry, Administration Manager, approaches Bill, his Senior Administration Clerk and says: 'I'm deeply unhappy with the way you are handling customer 'phone calls. I want you to sit by me and listen to the way I handle customers, because there's got to be an improvement in your attitude.'

How useful is this approach, on a scale of 1 to 5, where 1 is really useful and likely to produce excellent results; and 5 is not at all useful and not at all likely to produce excellent results?

(tick one box only)

1 ☐    2 ☐    3 ☐    4 ☐    5 ☐

Reason for your response

*Case study 2*

Caroline, Sales Manager, spends over an hour with Jon, one of the sales team, carefully explaining targets and planning learning activities. At the end of the discussion Jon confides that he doesn't think he can meet his targets and he's not at all sure about the training and learning that lie ahead for him.

Caroline says 'Well, targets are targets, and you're going to have to get on with it and meet them – that's what selling is all about. Look, Jon, I don't want to think I've wasted over an hour of my time on this ... you need the training, I've booked it and that's all there is to it.'

How useful is this approach, on a scale of 1 to 5, where 1 is really useful and likely to produce excellent results; and 5 is not at all useful and not at all likely to produce excellent results?

(tick one box only)
1 ❑     2 ❑     3 ❑     4 ❑     5 ❑

Reason for your response

*Case study 3*

Sam, Senior Partner in a law firm, offers to take Susan, a newly qualified solicitor, to a meeting with an important client so that she can gain an insight into the background of a particularly complex case. Susan acknowledges the offer, but says she would really prefer to spend the time looking through the files and then discussing her findings with Sam. He agrees to this.

How useful is this approach, on a scale of 1 to 5, where 1 is really useful and likely to produce excellent results; and 5 is not at all useful and not at all likely to produce excellent results?

(tick one box only)
1 ❑     2 ❑     3 ❑     4 ❑     5 ❑

Reason for your response

*Case study 4*

Barbara, Director of Human Resources, has been coaching Linda in negotiation skills for some time. Barbara now feels that it's time for Linda to try her wings in a real-life situation. They meet with a supplier to renegotiate a long-standing contract and Linda is in charge of the meeting. Linda achieves the deal she and Barbara had agreed but, when the supplier leaves, Barbara says 'You were really lucky to have got away with that! Why didn't you do what I told you to do? Stick to what I tell you next time!'

How useful is this approach, on a scale of 1 to 5, where 1 is really useful and likely to produce excellent results; and 5 is not at all useful and not at all likely to produce excellent results?

(tick one box only)
1 ☐    2 ☐    3 ☐    4 ☐    5 ☐

Reason for your response

## FEEDBACK

### Case study 1

This approach is not very useful as Bill is likely to feel demotivated and even resentful. A better approach would be for Gerry to say something like: 'I'm going to be dealing with customer 'phone calls this afternoon and I'd like you to sit in to give me some background on the customers. As a matter of fact, you might find it helpful to listen in, because I've noticed that you've had one or two problems with difficult customers. Hopefully, we can help each other this afternoon.'

### Case study 2

This approach is not very useful as it doesn't address the real problems, which are (a) why Jon doesn't think he can meet his targets and (b) why Jon is unsure about the training. A better approach would be for Caroline to say something like: 'I'm really glad that you felt you could mention this to me. What is it about your targets that concerns you most? Is it the quantity of sales, is it the time-frame, or is it something else?'

### Case study 3

This is a helpful approach because, although Susan isn't 'doing what Sam wants her to do', she is making a real commitment to learning. It may be that she understands her own learning style, and knows that she will gain more information from reading notes than she would from listening to a conversation. In the circumstances Sam shouldn't feel annoyed because his suggestion has not been accepted. He should recognize that Susan is taking real responsibility for getting to grips with a complex case.

**Case study 4**

This is not a helpful approach. Linda achieved the desired outcome, in her own way. Barbara's criticism (which is really about her own self-importance, rather than results), is neither useful nor relevant. A much better approach would be to say something like: 'Well done! You handled him really well. What made you decide to go with that approach, rather than the tactics we had agreed?' This would give Linda an opportunity to explain her thinking, at which point Barbara might (a) learn something herself or (b) be able to explain why Linda was fortunate on this occasion but why, on another occasion with a different person, Linda's approach might not work.

The most effective coaches tend also to be the most successful managers. They are people who:

- bring out the best in the individuals they manage
- encourage people to develop skills and abilities by giving them new experiences
- set challenging goals and targets for their people
- are tolerant of genuine mistakes (because they understand the learning cycle)
- provide encouragement, praise and support
- have the courage to take risks and delegate

# Preparing a coaching plan

Once you have identified that there needs to be an improvement in either skills, knowledge or attitude, your next step is to prepare a coaching plan which will enable the learner to close the gap between poor performance and good performance.

**ACTIVITY 27**

List three key items of information that a coaching plan should contain:

1

2

3

## FEEDBACK

Every coaching plan should contain the following key items of information:

- targets – the specific and measurable improvement you hope to achieve in performance, e.g. 'Tim to make a minimum of twenty-five sales calls each week'
- coaching technique(s) – details of the specific coaching techniques you plan to use in order achieve the targets you have set, e.g. 'discussion and work-shadowing'
- deadline – a specific time target by which the learning should have taken place, e.g. 'target to be achieved by 21 March 1997 (in three weeks)'
- monitoring and review – an outline of the way in which you intend to monitor and review progress with the learner, e.g. '(a) Check weekly log sheets; (b) Meet with Mike every Monday morning for three weeks to discuss progress; (c) Final meeting on 21 March to compare actual performance (log sheets) with target performance'

## ACTIVITY 28                                                                   C10.2, C10.4

Use this activity to prepare a coaching plan for two different members of staff.

> **Plan 1**
>
> Name:
>
> Job title:
>
> Aspect of performance for improvement:
>
> Improvement target:
>
> Deadline for improvement:
>
> Coaching technique(s):
>
> Method of monitoring and reviewing progress:

---

**Plan 2**

Name:

Job title:

Aspect of performance for improvement:

Improvement target:

Deadline for improvement:

Coaching technique(s):

Method of monitoring and reviewing progress:

---

## Summary

- The main aim of coaching is to develop people's work performance by:
  - delegating work that is complex, new, different, challenging or important
  - increasing the level of responsibility that someone assumes
  - providing the right environment and conditions in which someone can learn and practise new skills, knowledge and attitudes
- In circumstances where specific improvements are required from individual members of staff, coaching targets should be set. Coaching targets should be SMART:
  - **S**imple
  - **M**easurable
  - **A**chievable
  - **R**ealistic
  - **T**ime related
- Coaching techniques include providing opportunities for:
  - self-directed learning
  - observation of a demonstration by an expert
  - one-to-one discussion
  - team/group discussion
  - specific tasks/special projects
  - role-playing specific scenarios
  - work shadowing

- A coaching plan should contain the following information:
    - targets
    - coaching techniques to be used
    - deadline for completion
    - method of monitoring and reviewing progress

# Section 6   Mentoring

## Introduction

Many successful people can look back and acknowledge that, in some part, their current success is due to the assistance and support they received from a mentor at some point in their career.

'What does a Mentor actually do?' is the key question. Here are some definitions to give you an insight into the role of the mentor:

*Mentoring is a powerful system for making progress. It depends on the positive partnership of two people; a 'junior' partner, the mentee or protégé, who wants to get ahead and a 'senior' partner, the mentor, someone who is already ahead, who wants to help the junior learn the ropes[1].*

*To mentor can mean to:*

- *coach in management tasks and functions;*
- *befriend, support and counsel;*
- *help an individual towards personal growth;*
- *help a group develop and grow[2]*

*A good mentor provides personal/emotional support, personal feedback, emotional and intellectual challenge and a role model of someone who embodies many of the characteristics and skills that the [learner] seeks to develop[3]*

*A mentor is someone who helps another person to become what that person aspires to[4]*

In this section of the workbook we will be looking at the importance of the mentor/protégé relationship – both for the organization and for the individuals involved – and considering how you could make a positive contribution to the mentoring process within your company.

## The difference between a coach and a mentor

**Coaching** is usually about moving someone from 'can't do' or 'can't do very well' to 'can do' or 'can do it better now', and often involves the transfer of specific knowledge and skills from one person to another, most often in accordance with an agreed coaching plan. For example:

- 'I'll do it – you watch – then you copy what I do'
- 'Have a go at this task and see how you get on'
- 'Show me how you usually do it – OK – now try it this way'

**Mentoring** is a different approach altogether. The word Mentor comes from the Greek legend of Odysseus, who entrusted the welfare and training of his son to the goddess Athene. She transformed herself into human form as Mentor and became wise counsellor and helper to the boy while Odysseus was away on his travels.

The mentoring task involves sharing time and wisdom, and giving advice and direction. This process, when undertaken voluntarily and with a generous spirit, can often have a profoundly beneficial effect on others, both professionally and personally.

You have, almost certainly, at some point in your life, looked to a mentor for information, help, advice, encouragement and support. Right now, perhaps without even realizing it, you may be a mentor to a colleague at work. For example, if there is someone at work who:

- quizzes and questions you about how you might tackle a specific problem, or handle a specific situation
- tends to copy some aspect of your personality or presentation – the clothes you wear; the car you drive; the vocabulary you use; the approach you take to handling difficult situations
- gives the impression that they (genuinely) hold you in very high regard and, maybe, even think of you as the 'fount of all knowledge'
- often refer to your achievements, views or opinions when in conversation with others: 'Well, Sue Taylor thinks that ...'

then it could be that they regard you as their informal mentor.

### ACTIVITY 29

Consider the mentors you have had during your career to date. List three key tasks that those people have performed for you:

1

2

3

## FEEDBACK

Mentors assist their protégés by:

- providing insight – perhaps into the culture of the company; or into the 'politics' or economics of business life; or into the traditions that surround a particular profession
- providing continuous personal support
- acting as a confidential sounding board for hopes, fears and ambitions
- helping the learner to comes to terms with real-life problems, as they occur in the real world by offering the benefit of his or her practical experience
- demonstrating to the learner how, in business, theory relates to practice – 'forget the text books – this is what actually happens'
- acting as a role model

## CASE STUDY

Simon, a garage manager, describes his relationship with a mentor.

'Stan was my first boss – he owned the garage where I was employed as a very, very junior sales assistant. During the time I worked for him he taught me everything I know about cars, selling, life, relationships, money ... he was my boss, a good friend, a wonderful teacher and my role model. When he died and the firm closed down I was far more upset about losing Stan than I was about losing the job.'

## ACTIVITY 30

Consider the characteristics of a **good** mentor and a **poor** mentor, and then complete the chart below.

| Key characteristics of a GOOD mentor | Key characteristics of a POOR mentor |
| --- | --- |
| 1 | 1 |
| 2 | 2 |
| 3 | 3 |
| 4 | 4 |

## FEEDBACK

In response to the last activity you probably listed some of the following key characteristics:

GOOD mentors:

- consistently model the skills, attitudes and abilities to which the protégé aspires
- recognize the importance of personal and professional development, and share their knowledge and experience generously and willingly
- accept, totally, that there is more than one way to do something , and allow people the freedom to achieve the desired results in their own way, using their own methods
- demonstrate flexible attitudes and proactive behaviour – and encourage others to do the same
- provide supportive feedback on potential, abilities, strengths and areas where further development is needed

- offer recognition of effort and achievement

POOR mentors:

- seek to dominate their protégés and impose their own opinions, solutions, tactics or ideology – 'do as I do, think as I do, and you'll get on all right'
- use the role of mentor to work to their own agenda – for instance, exert undue influence on their protégés to encourage them to act in the best interests of the mentor (or their particular function), rather than the best interests of the protégé or the organization

- 'go through the motions' of being a mentor without any real commitment to the role
- adopt rigid, inflexible attitudes – 'we've always done it like this, and it's always worked before, so there's no reason to change things'
- assume that they are always right and they always know best
- offer judgemental rather than constructive criticism; biased rather than unbiased feedback
- harbour negative feelings – jealousy, bitterness or resentment – because, in their view, the protégé is enjoying benefits (perhaps the advantage of having a mentor) which they didn't have access to when they were climbing the ladder to success
- pay little or no attention to establishing and maintaining a good relationship with their protégé

# Establishing and maintaining a good working relationship

Within a formal mentoring programme, the key to success is the quality of the relationship between the mentor and their protégé. People – whether junior staff starting out on a career path or senior managers who have almost reached the top of the corporate ladder – are often likely to have some reservations about being assigned a mentor.

## ACTIVITY 31

For the purpose of this activity imagine that you have been told that a more senior manager has been assigned to you as your mentor, and that you are required to attend an initial meeting with this person to establish the ground rules. Consider the statements below and tick whichever could apply to you.

Prior to the initial meeting with my mentor I might feel:

|  | Yes |
|---|---|
| ■ Concerned that my mentor and I might not be able to establish a close working relationship | ❏ |
| ■ Apprehensive about issues of confidentiality | ❏ |
| ■ Unwilling to disclose too much too soon | ❏ |
| ■ Anxious that, perhaps, my mentor might have been 'rail roaded' into taking on this additional role, and so might be an unwilling participant in the programme | ❏ |
| ■ Worried about the way in which my progress on the mentoring programme might affect my status or career prospects within the company | ❏ |

|                                                                                    | Yes |
| ---------------------------------------------------------------------------------- | --- |
| ■ Anxious not to get into a conflict situation with my mentor                      | ❏   |
| ■ Concerned that my mentor might interfere in the way I do my job                  | ❏   |
| ■ Unwilling to reveal too many personal details                                    | ❏   |

## FEEDBACK

Your responses to this activity will, of course, be personal to you. However, most people who approach their first meeting their mentor are likely to experience many, if not all, of these concerns.

## CASE STUDY

Paul, a senior manager in merchant banking, explains how he felt when he was informed that he had been selected for inclusion in his company's mentoring programme.

'Quite soon after I joined this company I was told that the Vice-President was to be my mentor. I didn't know Steve at the time – from where I was standing he seemed to be a high-flying whiz-kid from New York and I couldn't see how we would be able to relate to one another, let alone work together in a fairly intimate relationship. In addition, I felt disadvantaged because he held such a senior position and, it seemed to me, that I'd be firmly in the spotlight and under the microscope. That didn't appeal to me at all. In the event, it actually worked very well and I learned a great deal from him. So much so that I applied for, and got, a job with the company at the head office in Boston. I was able to make the transition from working here at home in the UK to working in the US because I learned so much from Steve – both about our company and about the American way of doing business. So, a situation I initially perceived as potentially quite dangerous in fact turned out to be a golden opportunity.'

Mentors, too, sometimes feel as though they may have bitten off more than they can chew by volunteering to participate in the programme.

## ACTIVITY 32

1   Take a few minutes to identify any concerns you personally might have if you were asked to take on the role of mentor to someone in your organization. Note your ideas below.

Concerns I would have about taking on the role of mentor:

2   Now think about the benefits of undertaking this role within your organization.

Benefits I might enjoy as a result of taking on the role of mentor:

## FEEDBACK

Common **concerns** that mentors have before the mentoring process begins include:

- Is this going to take up too much of my time?
- How is this going to impact on my job performance?
- Is this person going to expect too much from me, in terms of time and energy?
- I'm not the right kind of person to be Agony Aunt, Counsellor and Problem Solver!

If you do decide to act as a mentor, (and this always works best when the mentors volunteer their services), make sure that you set clear boundaries for the relationship. You can do this by getting clear about:

- the amount of time, each week, you are prepared to devote to the task of being a mentor
- what level of personal involvement will be comfortable for you. For example:
    - would you be prepared to spend personal time with your protégé? Perhaps going for a drink or a meal after work, or visiting the gym or the golf-club together?
    - would you be happy for your protégé to have your home number so that they could call you in the evening or at the weekends?
    - as the relationship progresses, where would want to draw the line with regard to the discussion of personal topics – finance? relationships? religion? politics?

- would you feel more or less comfortable with a protégé of the opposite sex? If so, why? In what way would this impact on the mentoring relationship?
- what practical steps can you to take to make sure that your own role and responsibilities are not adversely affected by the additional tasks involved in the mentoring process?

Only you know the answers to these questions, and it is important that you address these issues before the mentoring programme gets under way.

**Benefits** to mentors include:

- having an opportunity to make a valuable contribution to your organization by helping to develop someone's potential
- increased personal self-confidence and self-esteem
- increased sense of personal achievement and job satisfaction
- opportunity to enhance your own existing skills, or develop new ones
- higher profile within your company
- access to new people, sources of information, resources
- enhanced prospects for promotion or career development

# Setting up a mentoring programme

Organizations run many different kinds of mentoring programmes, including:

- programmes for a specific group of people:
    - junior, middle or senior managers
    - women, ethnic or other minority groups
    - new recruits to the company
    - staff who are actively seeking career progression
    - teams who are about to undertake new projects
- programmes for specific purposes:
    - develop staff to enable them step into more senior roles
    - support staff at times when the organization is undergoing rapid or complex change
    - introduce self-managed learning
    - enable people to develop new and complex skills, e.g. European languages; working with advanced technology; undertaking negotiations in S.E. Asia
    - support managers who are undertaking specific kinds of training or learning activities, e.g. MBA by distance learning; NVQ level 4/5; NVQ Assessor Programme; part-time MA or MSc at a local university

## CHOOSING THE MENTORS

In most companies who run mentoring programmes, the mentors are chosen from volunteers at middle and senior management levels. (Companies who run these kinds of programmes include: Marks & Spencer plc; British Alcan Aluminium plc; TSB Bank plc; Brent Council; Trafalgar House Construction Ltd; South West Thames Regional Health Authority.)[5]

Mentors should be able to offer participants in the programme:

- in-depth knowledge and understanding of the business, profession or specialism in which the protégé is engaged (e.g. public relations, health care, architecture) plus a clear insight into the culture and workings of the company for which both mentor and protégé work
- a sincere belief that mentoring is a worthwhile and beneficial process for everyone involved
- good communication skills
- willingness to create rapport and establish a good working relationship
- ability to motivate and inspire
- respect, honesty, integrity, confidentiality and a commitment to ethical behaviour in all dealings between the mentor and the protégé

# Training the mentors

It really isn't sufficient to identify suitable mentors and then simply let them loose on an unsuspecting world. Anyone who is going to undertake the role of mentor should have some initial training and preparation so that they can carry out their role professionally, and to the very best of their ability.

**ACTIVITY 33**

For the purpose of this activity, imagine that you have been asked to create a one- or two-day training programme for the people who are going to act as mentors within your organization. List five topics you would present during the training:

1

2

3

4

5

**FEEDBACK**

All of the following topics could usefully be included in a mentors' training programme:

- what mentoring is, and what it is not
- the benefits of mentoring for the organization, and for everyone involved
- the role of the mentor
- mentor skills
- the qualities which a good mentor should possess, and the behaviours which should be avoided
- potential pitfalls and problems, and how to overcome them
- how long the mentoring process/relationship is likely to last
- ways in which the mentors can access guidance, support and encouragement for themselves (if the going gets tough)

# Organizing the programme

A mentoring programme can be organized in a variety of different ways, including any combination of the following:

- one-to-one meetings between mentor and protégé
- core group meetings attended by the protégés who are, maybe, at the same managerial level, or from the same department, function or unit, plus their mentors

- whole group meetings between all the protégés on the programme, plus all the mentors
- one-day training sessions
- weekend residential sessions
- informal 'get-togethers'

In addition, protégés' line managers (those who are not involved as mentors) may also be invited to attend some of the meetings as this helps to involve them, and keeps the lines of communication open.

Use the next activity to identify the strategy you might use to create and implement a mentoring programme within your organization.

**ACTIVITY 34**                                                                C10.4

Complete the chart below with information relevant to your organization.

| Within your current organization ... | |
|---|---|
| Which group of people would most benefit from being involved as protégés on a mentoring programme? | |
| Should the mentoring programme be undertaken with a specific objective in mind? If so, what should that objective be? | |
| What method should be used to motivate people to volunteer as mentors? | |
| What kind of selection process should be used to select mentors from the volunteer group? | |
| Who should be responsible for making the selections? | |
| Which person – or group of people – should be responsible for driving the mentoring programme through the organization? | |

| | |
|---|---|
| How, when and where should mentor training take place? | |
| Who should be responsible for mentor training? | |
| Who should be responsible for selecting the protégés? | |
| How, when and where should the protégés be introduced and inducted into the programme? | |
| Who should be responsible for protégé introduction and induction? | |
| What system should be used for monitoring success? | |
| Who should be responsible for monitoring success? | |
| How long should the programme last? | |
| What could your personal contribution be to the success of the programme? | |

# Summary

- Within most organizations the main purposes of mentoring programmes are to:
  - develop managers for more senior roles
  - introduce and support management of change
  - introduce self-managed learning
  - help to develop new or different skills
  - help personal and professional development
  - support managers undertaking education or training

- The mentoring task involves willingly:
  - sharing time and wisdom
  - providing guidance, advice, encouragement and support
  - helping people to achieve their full potential and climb the ladder to success
- Mentors can be of most assistance to their protégés by providing:
  - an insight into the profession, the business, the culture
  - continuous personal support
  - a non-critical, non-judgemental listening ear
  - practical links between theory and practice
  - the benefit of his/her experience to solve real-life problems
- Good mentors:
  - are a role model for best practice
  - generously share their knowledge and experience
  - allow people to operate in their own way
  - demonstrate flexible attitudes and proactive behaviour
  - provide constructive feedback
  - recognize effort and achievement
- Poor mentors:
  - attempt to dominate their protégés and impose their own ideas and opinions
  - use their role of mentor as an opportunity to advance their own agenda
  - adopt rigid and inflexible attitudes
  - assume they are always right
  - offer judgemental criticism and biased feedback
  - harbour jealousy, bitterness or resentment towards their protégé – because they are frightened that they might lose something if their protégé gains something from the mentoring programme
  - make little attempt to establish and maintain a good working relationship with their protégé
- Benefits to mentors include:
  - making a valuable contribution
  - increasing personal self-confidence and self-esteem
  - increasing sense of achievement and job satisfaction
  - enhancing existing skills and develop new ones
  - raising personal profile within the organization
  - accessing new people, information, resources
  - enhancing career development and promotion prospects
- Setting up a mentoring programme involves:
  - deciding which staff will participate as protégés
  - deciding the purpose of the programme
  - choosing the mentors who (ideally) should be given the opportunity to volunteer

- training the mentors
- introducing the protégés to the programme
- deciding on the format of meetings
- monitoring progress

## Notes

1 *Networking and Mentoring: A woman' guide*, by Dr Lily M. Segerman-Peck, Piatkus (1991).

2 'Mentoring is for Personal Growth', by Clare Freeman, in *Organisations and People*, October 1994, Vol. 1, no. 4, pp. 32–35.

3 'Mentoring for Success', by Margot Cairnes, in *The Practising Manager*, April 1995, vol. 15, no. 2, pp. 11–16.

4 *Mentoring: A Strategy for Learning in a Rapidly Changing Society*, Montreal CEGEP, John Abott College (1988).

5 List from *Management Directions – Mentoring*, by Bob Norton and Jill Tivey, Institute of Management (1955), pp. 5 and 26.

# Workbook summary

Now that you have completed the twelfth workbook in this series, you should feel sufficiently confident to be able to:

- take control of your own self-development and career planning
- design, deliver and assess training events
- coach staff to improve their job performance
- act as a mentor and wise adviser

In Workbook 13, *Building a High Performance Team*, we will be looking at the techniques for empowering and motivating the people on your team.

Topics that have been touched upon in this workbook are covered in greater depth in other books in this series:

- Workbook 2: *Managing Yourself*
- Workbook 7: *Improving your Organization's Success*
- Workbook 11: *Getting the Right People to do the Right Job*
- Workbook 14: *The New Model Leader*
- Workbook 16: *Communication*

# Recommended reading

Pedler, Mike, Burgoyne, John and Boydell, Tom (1978), *A Manager's Guide to Self-Development*, McGraw-Hill

Norton, Bob and Tivey, Jill (1995), *Management Directions – Mentoring*, Institute of Management

Taylor, David and Bishop, Sue (1994), *Readymade Activities for Developing Your Staff*, Institute of Management/Pitman Publishing

Hirsh, Wendy and Jackson, Charles (1994), *Successful Career Planning in a Week*, Institute of Management/Hodder & Stoughton

Carter, Stephen and Lewis, Gareth (1994), *Successful Mentoring in a Week*, Institute of Management/Hodder & Stoughton

Peel, Malcolm (1994), *Successful Training in a Week*, Institute of Management/ Hodder & Stoughton

Harrison, Rosemary (1988), *Training and Development*, Institute of Personnel Management

# About the Institute of Management

The mission of the Institute of Management (IM) is to promote the development, exercise and recognition of professional management.

The IM is the leading professional organization for managers. Its efforts and resources are devoted to ensuring the continuing development and success of its members.

At the forefront of management standards, the IM provides a range of services for its members. These include flexible training programmes and a unique range of support services such as career counselling, enquiry and research facilities and preferential prices on IM publications and other IM products.

Further details about the Institute of Management may be obtained from:

Institute of Management
Management House
Cottingham Road
Corby
Northants
NN17 1TT

Telephone 01536 204222

# We need your views

We really need your views in order to make the Institute of Management Open Learning Programme an even better learning tool for you. Please take time out to complete and return this questionnaire to Marketing Dept., Pergamon Flexible Learning, Linacre House, Jordan Hill, Oxford OX2 8DP.

Name:..................................................................................................................

Address:...............................................................................................................

............................................................................................................................

Title of workbook:...............................................................................................

If applicable, please state which qualification you are studying for. If not, please describe what study you are undertaking, and with which organization or college:

............................................................................................................................

Please grade the following out of 10 (10 being extremely good, 0 being extremely poor):

Content:         ..............     Suitability for ability level:         ..............

Readability:    ..............     Qualification coverage:              ..............

What did you particularly like about this workbook?

............................................................................................................................

Are there any features you disliked about this workbook? Please identify them.

............................................................................................................................

Are there any errors we have missed?
If so, please state page number: ...............................

How are you using the material? For example, as an open learning course, as a reference resource, as a training resource, etc.

............................................................................................................................

How did you hear about the Institue of Management Open Learning Programme?:

Word of mouth:         Through my tutor/trainer:         Mailshot:

Other (please give details):...................................................................................

Many thanks for your help in returning this form.

# Institute of Management Open Learning Programme

This programme comprises seventeen workbooks, each on a core management topic with the latest management thinking, as well as a *User Guide* and a *Mentor Guide*.

Designed for self study through open learning, the workbooks cover all management experience from team building to budgeting, from the skills of self management to manage strategically for organizational success.

| *TITLE* | *ISBN* | *Price* |
|---|---|---|
| *The Influential Manager* | 0 7506 3662 9 | £22.50 |
| *Managing Yourself* | 0 7506 3661 0 | £22.50 |
| *Getting the Right People to Do the Right Job* | 0 7506 3660 2 | £22.50 |
| *Understanding Business Process Management* | 0 7506 3659 9 | £22.50 |
| *Customer Focus* | 0 7506 3663 7 | £22.50 |
| *Getting TQM to Work* | 0 7506 3664 5 | £22.50 |
| *Leading from the Front* | 0 7506 3665 3 | £22.50 |
| *Improving Your Organization's Success* | 0 7506 3666 1 | £22.50 |
| *Project Management* | 0 7506 3667 X | £22.50 |
| *Budgeting and Financial Control* | 0 7506 3668 8 | £22.50 |
| *Effective Financial and Resource Management* | 0 7506 3669 6 | £22.50 |
| *Developing Yourself and Your Staff* | 0 7506 3670 X | £22.50 |
| *Building a High Performance Team* | 0 7506 3671 8 | £22.50 |
| *The New Model Leader* | 0 7506 3672 6 | £22.50 |
| *Making Rational Decisions* | 0 7506 3673 4 | £22.50 |
| *Communication* | 0 7506 3674 2 | £22.50 |
| *Successful Information Management* | 0 7506 3675 0 | £22.50 |
| *User Guide* | 0 7506 3676 9 | £22.50 |
| *Mentor Guide* | 0 7506 3677 7 | £22.50 |
| Full set of workbooks plus *Mentor Guide* and *User Guide* | 0 7506 3359 X | £370.00 |

To order: *(Please quote ISBNs when ordering)*

- College Orders: 01865 314333
- Account holders: 01865 314301
- Individual Purchases: 01865 314627

*(Please have credit card details ready)*

For further information or to request a full series brochure, please contact: Management Marketing Department on: 01865 314459